THE BATTLE

OF

NEW GARDEN

NORTH CAROLINA FRIENDS HISTORICAL SOCIETY
P.O. Box 8502, Greensboro, NC 27419

NORTH CAROLINA YEARLY MEETING OF FRIENDS
5506 W. Friendly Avenue, Greensboro, NC 27410

THE BATTLE
OF
NEW GARDEN

ALGIE I. NEWLIN

Library of Congress Catalog Card Number: 77-82787
ISBN 0–942–72726–6

Cover design by Gayle Fishel.

Cover photo by Tom Lassiter: detail of untitled watercolor
of Tarleton's dragoons in pursuit by artist Don Troiani
in collection of Guilford Courthouse National Military Park.

Maps by Fred Hughes.

Composition by Friendly Desktop Publishing.

Printed by Thomson–Shore.

1.5 M

TABLE OF CONTENTS

PREFACE

After entering Guilford College as a freshman I heard vague references to a battle which took place on the morning before the Battle of Guilford Courthouse around New Garden Meetinghouse and along the road which is now the western border of the campus of Guilford College. Equally alluring was the fascinating story of the red finger prints which in some devious manner were transferred from the hands of the soldiers wounded in this and the Battle of Guilford Courthouse to the ceiling of the old frame meetinghouse which stood in the middle of the New Garden cemetery until 1876. In addition to these stories from tradition, I saw, in New Garden cemetery, the black marble monument, erected around 1908 near the Revolutionary Oak, marking a grave in which both American and British soldiers were buried.

There is little doubt that these references to events of the Revolutionary War which took place near the scenes of my college days fired my interest in these events whose history seemed hopelessly lost. For four decades I taught the history of the United States and of North Carolina in a classroom overlooking the scenes of some of the fighting. I often felt the urge to hunt down the narrative of this phantom battle. Since my retirement from teaching I have given much time to collecting and collating the available material which has bearing on that morning battle. My familiarity with the surrounding country and with the grounds on which the actions took place has facilitated the work of bringing the narrative to life. Fortunately, most of the material which has gone into this treatise was found near at hand in numerous sources in the Library of Guilford College.

Algie I. Newlin
Professor Emeritus of History, deceased
Guilford College
Greensboro, North Carolina

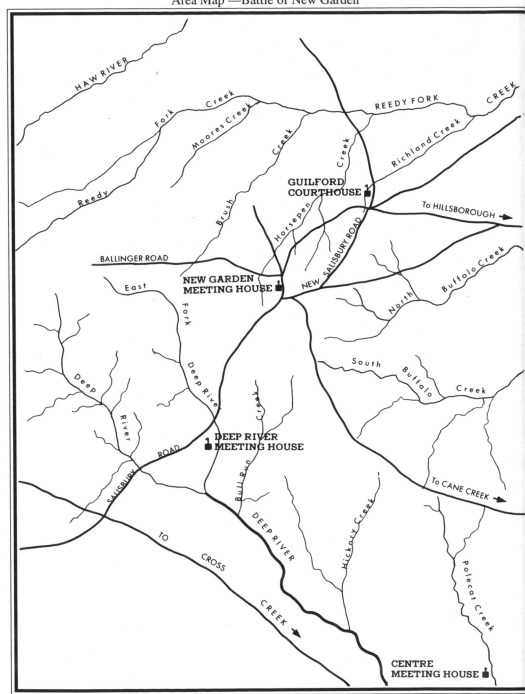

Map by Fred Hughes

Detail of Area Map —Battle of New Garden

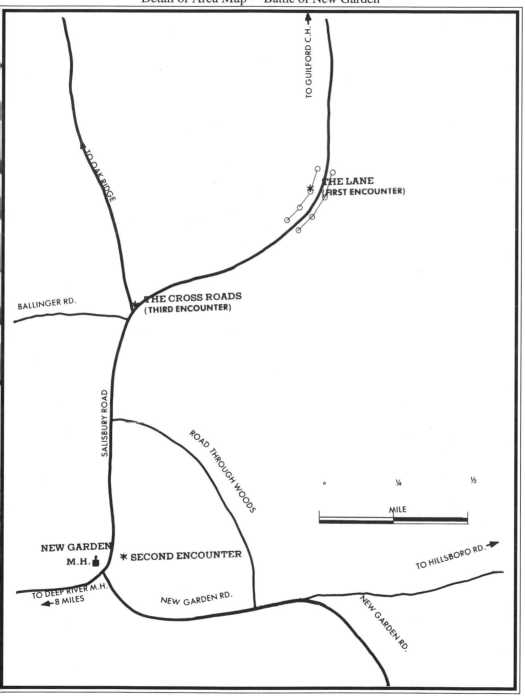

THE BATTLE OF NEW GARDEN

The Battle of New Garden occurred on the morning of March 15, 1781, a few hours before the Battle of Guilford Courthouse, four and one–half miles away. It has never received the attention which it deserves in the general history of North Carolina or in the history of the Revolutionary War in that state; nor has it ever been honored with a name. The best that history has done for it is to refer to it as a skirmish between American and British cavalry units just before the Battle of Guilford Courthouse. This neglect is surprising once one comes to appreciate the magnitude and duration of the action.

The Battle of New Garden began about sunrise, or soon thereafter, and filled most of the morning. The Battle of Guilford Courthouse began about one o'clock in the afternoon and lasted for two hours. The first shots of the morning were fired near New Garden Meetinghouse. Instead of a single, minor cavalry skirmish to which history has generally limited it there were three distinct, sharp encounters fought in succession between sizable units of the two armies which included infantry as well as cavalry. Though this action occurred on the same day and near the site of the Battle of Guilford Courthouse, there are reasons for treating it as a separate battle, and these will be given later.

Suggesting a name for a battle which has gone nameless for nearly two hundred years may smack of presumption, but this narrative seems to demand it. The first shots of the day, and one of the most hotly contested battles of the morning, occurred on the road and grounds around New Garden Friends Meetinghouse.* All of the encounters of the morning battle took place along a segment of the Old Salisbury

---

* *Reprint editor's note: members of the Religious Society of Friends, founded by George Fox in England in the 1650s, called their "churches" meetinghouses. Members were and are called Friends or Quakers.*

Road, known then and now as New Garden Road. For these reasons it seems appropriate to suggest that all of the morning's encounters be considered collectively as the Battle of New Garden. Since so little is known about the battle, a brief descriptive statement pinpointing its place within the American Revolution, along with a short outline of the sequence of events in the morning conflict, may be of assistance to the reader as he or she attempts to follow the narrative of the rapidly changing drama of that morning.

A chronology of the Revolutionary War reveals that it may be treated in two main stages: the first fought in the North and the second in the South. Of course, there were conflicts in both the North and the South which do not fit within the time limits set by this classification, but they are not of sufficient significance to mar seriously this division of the history of the war.

The Revolutionary War began at Lexington, Massachusetts on April 15, 1775, and it may be said that the first stage of the war ended with the Battle of Monmouth in New Jersey on June 28, 1778. During the year 1777, the British attempted to implement a master plan to end the war, making use of a three–pronged drive to divide the colonies with a military cordon along the Hudson Valley. This was intended to isolate New England and facilitate its conquest. After conquering this area, the British hoped to move south with greater force. This well–planned campaign came to a sudden end when the main British force was defeated and captured at Saratoga in June 1777. The British then evacuated Philadelphia and concentrated their forces in the seaport bases of Boston and New York.

With the failure of their northern campaign, the British turned to the South with a master plan for taking the southern states one by one, beginning with Georgia, the most southern and weakest of the thirteen. Savannah was captured on December 29, 1778. The conquest of the remainder of Georgia was completed soon thereafter. Charleston, the next primary objective, was not taken until May 12, 1780. Its capture was a serious blow to the independence movement in the South, as Charleston was the principal seaport in the South. Through it the British controlled much of the economic life of South Carolina. In taking Charleston the British also captured the largest American army in the South, variously estimated to have numbered between 3,500 and 5,000 men. With the British in control of Charleston and Savannah and much of the interior of Georgia and South Carolina, the Whig cause in the South was at a low ebb. At this point, the Continental Congress chose General Horatio Gates, to whom a British army had surrendered at Saratoga, to take command of the American forces in the South. Under his leadership, an American army was decimated in the Battle of Camden, South Carolina on August 16, 1780. The disaster at Camden, following that at Charleston by only three months, left little military strength in the Carolinas to meet expanding British forces.

The British now seemed ready to mount their drive into North Carolina. Their plan was that the main army under Lord Charles Cornwallis would sweep across the interior of North Carolina and draw Tory recruits along the way. To secure a base of supply for the invasion, a force would also be sent to occupy Wilmington, North Carolina at the mouth of the Cape Fear River. This stream was navigable as far inland as Cross Creek (now Fayetteville). To protect the invading army from the potentially strong Whigs in the western part of North Carolina, Major Patrick Ferguson was directed to lead his army of approximately 1,000 Loyalists in that direction. He made dire threats of drastic action if the Whigs should make any move toward the British. His boastful defiance stirred the Whigs to assemble in sufficient force to drive Ferguson back into South Carolina to the top of King's Mountain where he and all his men were either killed or captured on October 7, 1780.

It was as this point in the war that General Washington selected Nathanael Greene to replace the discredited General Gates and take command of the American forces in the South. In December 1780, Greene took command of what he called "the shadow of an American army in the midst of distress."

In January 1781, Lord Cornwallis sent his trusted cavalry leader, Lieutenant Colonel Banastre Tarleton, to destroy the western wing of General Greene's army. Daniel Morgan who was in command of this contingent of the American forces chose "Hannah's Cowpens" as the ground on which to meet Tarleton's attack. This place was located about twenty–five miles southwest of King's Mountain, and there on January 17, 1781, the American force came near to destroying Tarleton's army. The remnant, which escaped death or capture, fled with Colonel Tarleton in the lead. The Whig victories at King's Mountain and Cowpens, even though they were not major battles, gave the supporters of independence a tremendous boost in morale, but they had little if any effect on Greene's efforts to attract Whig recruits to his ragtag army.

A few days after the Battle of Cowpens, a British force commanded by Major James Craig landed at the mouth of the Cape Fear River and captured Wilmington with relative ease. This gave Cornwallis a much needed supply base for his invasion of the back country of North Carolina, provided the British could keep control of the Cape Fear River and the roads from Cross Creek to their army.

These developments prepared the way for one of the longest and one of the most striking campaigns of the Revolutionary War: a running battle between General Greene's small, loosely organized army and the small but battle–hardened and well–disciplined army commanded by Lord Cornwallis. The objective of each commander was to maneuver into a position from which he could destroy or seriously cripple the opposing army. In the process each hoped to make such a show of force that recruits would flock to his standard. In the race out of South Carolina, across North Carolina and into Virginia, General Greene did not gain sufficient strength for a full–scale battle with the British, but he made what has been called a "masterful retreat" in keeping out of reach of the hard–driving British army. In this race the British commander was outrun and out generaled, and was never able to force Greene into battle. When Cornwallis reached the Dan River in Virginia to find all of the American soldiers and their boats on the opposite side of the stream, he abandoned his pursuit of Greene's army and moved to Hillsborough in Orange County, North Carolina, where he issued a warm invitation to the Loyalists to join him in his effort to restore the province to the British Empire.

During the following month the two commanders kept their armies within a few miles of one another, continued their hit–and–run attacks, and maneuvered for position and strength from which to mount a showdown battle. The cavalry and the light infantry of the two armies were almost constantly on the move foraging for badly needed supplies, ready always to pounce upon exposed bands of the opposing army.

The whole campaign suggests that it was a war of attrition which hurt the British more than the Americans. It has been estimated that there were 137 battles, skirmishes, and raids during the two–month campaign. This alone justifies calling the campaign a running battle.

During this time the British army was gradually losing men, its supplies were diminishing, and it was being drawn farther and farther from its seaport base.

In the first few days of March 1781, General Greene's situation became more favorable. Recruits and supply wagons poured into his camp. He grew certain that his army had become strong enough to give the British the battle they had been seeking. He was also convinced that the battle should take place immediately, because the term of enlistment of many of the men in his militia would soon expire. These circumstances caused Greene to move his army to a position near Guilford Courthouse and, in effect, to throw down the gauntlet to Cornwallis, then only twelve miles away at Deep River Meetinghouse near Jamestown. Both armies were on the old Salisbury Road. New Garden Meetinghouse and the New Garden community lay between them.

The Battle of New Garden and the Battle of Guilford Courthouse came near the end of this historic running battle between Greene and Cornwallis. It occurred approximately seven months before the surrender of Cornwallis at Yorktown which virtually brought the war to an end. The Battle of New Garden may be seen as the last in the long series of conflicts between the forces of Greene and Cornwallis which led up to the Battle of Guilford Courthouse. On March 13th, Cornwallis moved his army to Deep River Friends Meetinghouse between the forks of Deep River. On the following day Greene's army occupied the ground around Guilford Courthouse and made plans to meet the British there in an all-out test of strength. These maneuvers inadvertently set the stage for the unforeseen Battle of New Garden.

In the histories of the Revolutionary War in North Carolina there is usually the implication that there was only one minor skirmish between cavalry units on the morning before the Battle at the Courthouse. However, two references have been found to three encounters at that time. In one of these, Colonel Henry Lee is quoted as saying there were three encounters.[1] The other reference is from the journal of an officer in a Delaware regiment which figured prominently in the afternoon battle.[2] Much of the material relative to the morning conflicts falls into place around these three encounters.

Near sunrise, pickets of the vanguard of the two armies started the morning conflict by firing at each other near New Garden Meetinghouse. Following this exchange of shots the three battles of the morning took place in rather rapid succession: the first near the entrance to the Jefferson Standard Country Club;* the next on the ground around New Garden Meetinghouse; and the third at the junction of Ballinger and New Garden Roads, generally known as the "Cross Roads."

One might ask then why we should not consider the Battle of New Garden as the first stage in the Battle of Guilford Courthouse? This is a logical question, for the close association with the major battle is obvious. If General Greene had not deployed his army near Guilford Courthouse and, in effect, challenged Cornwallis to attack him there, the Battle of New Garden would not have taken place. However, there are specific reasons why it may be considered a separate conflict. General Greene had a definite plan for the Battle at Guilford Courthouse. The battle which filled a good part of the morning had no place in that plan and did not change it in any way. It might be argued that the Battle of New Garden was preliminary to the battle at the Courthouse, and for that reason should be considered as a part of the major battle. But for that matter, all of the previous encounters in the long race between Greene and Cornwallis might then also be considered preliminary to the Battle of Guilford Courthouse. Ultimately, the principal distinction between the Battle of New Garden and these other earlier encounters is that New Garden was near Guilford Courthouse both in time and distance.

CIRCUMSTANCES LEADING TO THE BATTLE

What induced the American and British forces to carry out a bloody action in the middle of a peaceful Quaker community along their main road, in front of their homes, and around their meetinghouse on the morning of March 15, 1781? Coincidence resulting from two major circumstances of statewide significance brought the two armies together at just that time and place. One circumstance was the attitude of the people of North Carolina at that time, and the other was the geography of the area. By March 1781,

---

* *Reprint editor's note: now Jefferson Pilot Club.*

the political and military atmosphere of the back country of North Carolina was pushing Lord Cornwallis and General Greene toward a full–scale test of one another's strength. Each commander was convinced that large segments of the area's population could be drawn to the side which made a strong show of strength, and both commanders had been waging a psychological battle for the minds and support of the people of the area through which they passed as they raced across North Carolina.

Before leaving South Carolina, Cornwallis had become convinced that there was strong Loyalist sentiment in North Carolina and that a show of British force in the interior of the state would induce a large number of Loyalists to join his army:

> I was determined to fight the Rebel Army if it approached me, being convinced that it would be impossible to succeed in the object of our arduous Campaign—the calling forth of numerous loyalists of North Carolina—whilst a doubt remained in their minds of the superiority of our Army. With these views, I moved to the Quakers meeting, in the fork of Deep River, on the 13th, and on the 14th received the information which occasioned the movement which brought on the action at Guilford. . . .[3]

Colonel Tarleton similarly observed, ". . . the British troops would never expect great assistance from the Loyalists till they had destroyed Greene, and acquired a marked superiority in arms."[4] And Colonel Lee said that "General Greene's objects were to maintain a footing in North Carolina; and overawe the loyalists, and rouse the republicans."[5]

The ultimate stake in the campaign between the two armies was the control of North Carolina. Both commanders expected this to come from the contest between the two armies, if and when that could obtain. General Greene said: "If Ld. Cornwallis knows his true interest he will pursue our army. If he can dispose with that, he completes the reduction of the state."[6]

It is quite possible that the reluctance of Whigs to join Greene's army during the retreat to the north was due in part to their low estimate of the strength of his force, compounded by his inability to resist the advancing British force. On the other hand, the almost constant pestering of the British forces by the American cavalry and light troops and the failure of the British to strike the main American army kept the

Loyalists from joining the British in large numbers.

The British army was in a precarious position. It was more than 150 miles from its supply base in Wilmington, and it was experiencing great difficulty in obtaining sufficient food through foraging. Much of the army's distress was due to the near constant shadowing of the British forces by the American cavalry and light infantry. The seriousness of the situation was recognized in one British history of that period which observed that "the grievous distresses of the army, which were now become nearly unsupportable, under want of supplies of every species" [7] were serious threats to its existence. In addition to a shortage of food, shoes and other items of clothing were lacking or in poor condition. In the kind of war now being waged against them, the British were losing. In the month of February alone, the army's rolls showed a loss of 227 men — a serious loss for any army of less than 2,500 men. This accumulation of adversities would eventually bring defeat unless the Americans could be dealt a crippling blow.

The critical state of the British army and an appreciable influx of recruits and supplies into the American camp during the first few days of March gave General Greene the confidence to risk a battle. On their retreat across North Carolina, the two divisions of Greene's army had come together at Guilford Courthouse. The American commander is said to have considered this a favorable place for a duel with the British at that time, and the terrain to the west of the courthouse favored the American forces.

There was an additional reason for choosing this place to make a stand: there were several roads converging on Guilford Courthouse. These provided much needed avenues for the receipt of recruits and supplies and for retreat should that become necessary. The main thoroughfare through the area was the Great Road from Virginia to Salisbury. Guilford Courthouse, Deep River Meetinghouse, and New Garden Meetinghouse were all on this road. The British had to use it to reach the American forces from their camp between the forks of Deep River.

On the opposite side of the river from Deep River Meetinghouse, the Salisbury Road crossed a road connecting Salem and Cross Creek. Contemporary military accounts refer to this road as the "Deep River Road," since it paralleled that river. It constituted an important link in the British line of communications with their base in Wilmington and in their line of retreat should that prove necessary.

There were other roads which the American and British forces would use during and near the time of the battle. A road from Hillsborough passed through the watershed of North Buffalo Creek and connected with the Salisbury Road at Guilford Courthouse. From Buffalo Creek there was a narrow road which connected with the Salisbury Road at New Garden Meetinghouse. New Garden Road crossed streams and low places where the road would not support heavy traffic in rainy seasons. A new Salisbury Road had been constructed through the McAdoo Woods, along the ridge between the Buffalo Creek and Horsepen Creek watersheds, to provide an all–weather route around the difficult places on New Garden Road. This route approximated that of the present day Westridge Road.[8]

A road which was evidently a short cut from the Cross Roads on New Garden Road to the road from Buffalo Creek to New Garden Meetinghouse was used on one occasion by Colonel Tarleton in a hasty retreat from pursuit by Colonel Lee. It must have branched off from New Garden Road near the present parking lot of Guilford College and extended across the campus near King Hall and Archdale Hall and between the college's two athletic fields. The imprint of an old road, now visible in the woods to the east of the Armfield Athletic Center, is believed to have been a part of it.[9]

Time was also a factor in bringing on the battle. The growing strain on the British army made it imperative that the battle be fought as soon as possible. The increasing strength of the American army made it even more imperative. The American army had to be defeated quickly if the British army was to survive. General Greene became convinced that he had sufficient strength to meet the British, and on March 14th he moved his army from Speedwell Ironworks[10] on Troublesome Creek to Guilford Courthouse to await the British attack. He did not have long to wait.

The Men Who Fought

The Quaker inhabitants of the New Garden community must have stood in silent dread as dawn broke on the morning of March 15, 1781. Prospects for the day were ominous. Everyone must have known that the two armies poised on either side of them were ready for a bloody battle. Perhaps few, if any, of them had ever heard of the Ides of March, yet, they must have sensed a fatalism which characterizes that day. Throughout the morning, from sunrise until almost noon, hostile forces maneuvered, charged, fought, and retreated along New Garden Road near their homes. Tradition pictures some of these Quakers at a safe distance, watching as much of the spectacle as they could. They were seeing battle–hardened soldiers led by officers highly skilled in the type of warfare being waged in the southern campaign.

The leaders of the two contingents pitted against each other in the morning battle were the two most noted cavalry officers of the Revolutionary War. Lieutenant Colonel Henry Lee led the Americans and Lieutenant Colonel Banastre Tarleton led the British. Colonel Lee had won the favor of General Washington before coming south. Now he was enjoying similar recognition from Nathanael Greene. At the end of the campaign against Cornwallis, Greene said of Lee, "I am more indebted to this officer, than to any other for the advantage gained over the enemy, in the operations of the last campaign." [11] Colonel Tarleton was a favorite of his commander, Lord Cornwallis, before they entered the southern area in 1779.

These two young officers are universally recognized as the most colorful cavalry leaders in the Revolutionary War. For more than two months they had been matching their military genius against one another and meeting the exigencies of the tortuous military campaign with such consummate skill as to develop their type of hit–and–run warfare almost to a science. By foraging, scouting, raiding, sniping, maneuvering, and skirmishing they had brought the men under their command to a peak of mental and physical preparation for the slashing attacks which took place along New Garden Road. [12]

Throughout the morning, Lee and Tarleton dashed from one focal point to another, shouting orders and participating in the fighting. Riding as "Light Horse Harry" Lee and "Bloody" Tarleton, they readily caught the eye of history. These bitter rivals were much alike, though both would have been infuriated by the comparison. They were young, handsome, wellborn, educated, proud, vain, rugged, indomitable, and at times ruthless. The Lee family had already become well–known in Virginia. Young Henry Lee was a Princeton man and he had planned to study law — but the war caught up with him. Tarleton was an Oxford dropout who had found athletics more appealing than the books and lectures which might have become stepping stones to a career in the legal profession. He was the son of John Tarleton, the "Great T," mayor of Liverpool, who had made a fortune in the West Indian slave trade.[13]

Both of these handsome blades had a flare for showmanship and for smartness in dress. Their eighteenth century sartorial trappings might well be the envy of any fashionable young man of the 1970s. Colonel Tarleton wore a snug fitting jacket, which artist Joshua Reynolds pictured in green, with tight fitting white linen breeches, black boots, and heavy spurs. For a headdress he wore either a helmet adorned with a plume or a low–crowned, plumed hat.[14] His long hair was tied at the back of his neck. Physically he was "a perfect model of manly strength and vigor."[15]

Lee matched his archrival in almost every respect. His dress, physique, temperament, and vanity were certainly equal to that of Tarleton's. He had a keen eye for horses and would ride none but the finest the country could offer. Exception was made only when his charger threw him in the heat of battle; then he would ride what he could get.

When Lee and Tarleton clashed at New Garden they were of college age —"boy colonels." Lee had just passed his twenty–fifth birthday, and Tarleton was twenty–six. However, their youth and dress may be deceptive. Their *rencontre* on the ground around New Garden Meetinghouse and along New Garden Road was neither a strutting contest nor a drama rehearsal. They met with "blood in the eye," to square off a bitter rivalry which had begun four years earlier at the Spread Eagle Tavern near Valley Forge where Tarleton's plan to capture Lee turned into a defeat which nearly cost the brash young Englishman his life. When he finally reached safety, his helmet had been shot away, his jacket had been punctured with bullet holes, and his horse had been wounded three times.[16] At Guilford Courthouse, the armies of Cornwallis and Greene were out to destroy each other; at New Garden neither Lee nor Tarleton had any other objective.

Throughout this phase of the war in the South the stakes were high, the outcome uncertain, the nerves taut. At times, when the end seemed to justify the means, atrocities were committed. Two instances of this are notable: one in the Waxhaw region when Tarleton's men are reputed to have sabered to death a company of Whigs who were in the act of surrender;[17] the other (often called Pyle's Hacking Match) at

21

Holt's Farm in what is now Alamance County, North Carolina, when Lee's men hacked to death nearly one hundred Loyalist recruits commanded by Colonel John Pyle who mistook their green–coated assailants for friendly British cavalry. Nearly one third of the men of the Tory regiment had been killed while most of the remaining two hundred had been wounded still pleading that a horrible mistake was being made and appealing for a cessation of the attack.[18] While "Tarleton's Quarters" haunted the British Legion after the affair in the Waxhaws, the massacre of Colonel Pyle's regiment a few weeks later left Lee's American Legion with a similar stigma. A month before the Battle of New Garden, Colonel Lee's bugler was killed near Oak Ridge by some of Tarleton's Mounted troops. Lee was so enraged by this act that he ordered hot pursuit of the Tories and shouted, "Give them no quarters! Kill the last of them." [19] These incidents provide some indication of the spirit which drove the opposing forces as they fought each other in the Battle of New Garden. Moreover, since Colonel Tarleton's cavalry was composed largely of Tories, the question arises as to whether the fighting at New Garden was made more bitter by the fact that the conflict was between Tories and Whigs.

In the Battle of New Garden, the leaders and the men under their command were all well trained and fully battle–hardened for hit–and–run warfare. The mounted troops of Lee's Legion have been called "the best cavalry in North America" at the time.[20] In addition to cavalry, Lee's troops included riflemen from the mountains of North Carolina and Virginia commanded by Colonel William Campbell, brother–in–law of Patrick Henry. Campbell had commanded the mountain militia when they annihilated the army of Major Patrick Ferguson at Kings Mountain.

After his crippling defeat at Cowpens, Tarleton's cavalry had been brought back to full strength by Loyalist recruits from South Carolina. Their horses were drawn from the farms of the area and were considered inferior to the Pennsylvania and Virginia horses of the American cavalry. However, Colonel Tarleton's men were highly disciplined. The men of the American Legion were reluctant to disparage their fighting ability.

The two German regiments with Tarleton had already won renown and they would distinguish themselves further at Guilford Courthouse. Both regiments were in the battles at New Garden Meetinghouse and at the Cross Roads. The men of the Twenty–third Regiment of Colonel

Webster's Brigade who were instrumental in turning the tide at the Cross Roads were the famous "Welsh Fusiliers," formerly identified as the regiment of the Prince of Wales. The men of Webster's Brigade have been called the "most seasoned" regulars in the army of Cornwallis.[21]

It is not possible to give an accurate enumeration of the British and American men in the Battle of New Garden. If any record of their numerical strength was ever made, it has not been found. Traditions, statements of eyewitnesses, and estimates of the composition of the two armies made before and at the time of the Battle of Guilford Courthouse have been examined. Tradition indicates that the two forces which fought each other during the morning of the 15th were about equal. Immediately this raises the question of whether this equality was limited to the battle around New Garden Meetinghouse. There is clear evidence that the British pushed reinforcements into the battle at the Cross Roads in sufficient numbers to upset the balance.

Contemporary estimates have been preserved by Addison Coffin, who had lived within view of New Garden Road and near to the scene of some of the fighting. Forty years after the battle, he interrogated a man who participated in the fighting along New Garden Road, residents of the community who had witnessed the battle at the Cross Roads, and persons who had helped to bury the dead along New Garden Road and on the battlefield at the Courthouse. As a result of these inquiries Coffin was led to say, "Campbell and Lee, with less than 600 riflemen [sic], delayed Cornwallis three hours, compelling him to deploy 2,000 men into [the] line of battle to dislodge and drive them from the woods in which they were posted." [22] I have found no other account to corroborate this evaluation of the strength of the British force at the Cross Roads, but this estimate will be given further consideration when the battle at the Cross Roads is treated in more detail.

Colonel Lee indicated that on the morning of March 15th he had under his command not only his own Legion (which included both cavalry and infantry), but also the militia commanded by Colonel James Preston[23] and Colonel William Campbell. It appears that Colonel Preston and his force were under the command of Colonel Campbell during the battle, even though Preston's regiment was larger than Campbell's. In Lee's account of the battle in the Lane, Captain Armstrong's company figures prominently.[24] For a list of the units commanded by Colonel Lee in the morning battles and maneuvers, the following tabulation may be approximately correct:

Colonel James Preston 300
Colonel William Campbell 60
Colonel Lee's Cavalry 75
Colonel Lee's Infantry 82
Captain John Armstrong's Co 100
        Total 617

David Schenck believed that Colonel Preston's force did not exceed 200.[25] This would reduce Colonel Lee's total to 517, placing the estimate a little below that made by Addison Coffin.

A search for information on the strength of the units commanded by Colonel Tarleton leads one through some of the same sources consulted for estimates of the strength of Lee's command. On March 2nd, nearly two weeks before the battle, the units commanded by Tarleton consisted of "the cavalry, a few mounted infantry, the light company of guards and one hundred and fifty men of Colonel Webster's Brigade." [26] When the British army moved out of its camp at Deep River Meetinghouse to begin the march to Guilford Courthouse, Colonel Tarleton says:

> The main body at daybreak marched toward the enemy's camp. The cavalry, the light infantry of the guards and the yagers composed the advanced guard. Colonel Webster's brigade, the Bose regiment, and the brigade of the guard followed successively; . . .[27]

This arrangement of the troops for the march toward Guilford Courthouse had been ordered by Cornwallis.[28] Tarleton commanded the advance guard. The Bose regiment and men from Webster's brigade are known to have been with Tarleton in the battles on New Garden Road. They were directly behind the advance guard in the line of march indicated above. Lieutenant von Trott of the Bose regiment was mortally wounded in the battle around New Garden Meeting-house, an indication that this Hessian regiment was with Tarleton in that conflict. The Twenty–third Regiment of Webster's Brigade played an important role in the battle at the Cross Roads. Estimates of the personnel of the different units with Colonel Tarleton in the Battle of New Garden reveal the following:

Tarleton's Legion (cavalry and infantry 174
The Yagers 97
The Bose Regiment 313
The Twenty–third Regiment .... <u>258</u>
        Total 842

This total is for the final battle at the Cross Roads after the Twenty–third Regiment had joined Tarleton's corps. Since it was not at the battle at New Garden Meetinghouse, the number of British soldiers in that encounter must have been 584, which approximates the estimate made from tradition.

COLONEL LEE MISLEADS HISTORIANS

Colonel Lee and Colonel Tarleton eventually published their respective accounts of the Southern Campaign. These two books are valuable sources on the war in the South. Colonel Lee's *Memoirs* furnish more information about the events in the Battle of New Garden than any other source, but they contain an error, repeated several times, about the location of New Garden Meetinghouse. This has misled some historians down to the present. In giving a description of the fighting he wrote the following footnote:

> This was not New Garden meetinghouse. Which was twelve miles from Guilford [Courthouse] and from which Cornwallis had moved from dawn of day. It was now about an hour after sunrise — "the sun had risen just above the trees:" and Cornwallis in his report says this affair happened four miles from Guilford; that is about eight miles from New Garden meetinghouse. Colonel Howard confirms this estimate of distance, for he says the firing was distinctly heard at Guilford. It was probably a meetinghouse of less notoriety than that at New Garden.[29]

Colonel Lee was clearly in error. The meetinghouse which he considered "of less notoriety" was New Garden. He thought Deep River Meetinghouse was New Garden. Every one of his references to New Garden Meetinghouse should be translated "Deep River Meetinghouse." Reverse the names of the meetinghouses, and the distances which he gives are approximately correct. If he had consulted Mouzon's map of North and South Carolina, published just before the outbreak of the war, he would have found New Garden Meetinghouse, properly named and located. The map gives Deep River Meetinghouse properly placed between the forks of Deep River, but designated only as "Quakers meetinghouse." Cornwallis had this map,[30] and in his report on the events leading to the battle he said, "I had moved to the Quaker's meeting on the forks of the Deep River on the 13th."[31] This identification is the same as that on the map. General Greene and Colonel Tarleton used the same reference to Deep River Meetinghouse.

Colonel Lee's confusing of the names of the two meetinghouses seems strange, for he was around each one of them enough to have learned their names. He was in a stiff battle on the ground around New Garden Meetinghouse, passed there several times and seemed well acquainted with the roads in that vicinity. He had also spent much time shadowing the British army around Deep River Meetinghouse both before and after the Battle of Guilford Courthouse. In reporting the events after the Battle of Guilford Courthouse, he repeated the error twice: once when he implied that the British camped at New Garden for the first night after leaving Guilford Courthouse, and again when a letter written to General Greene indicated that he was writing from New Garden.[32] In both instances it is evident that he was referring to Deep River Meetinghouse. Lord Cornwallis and Colonel Tarleton, on the other hand, indicated that the British camped at Deep River rather than at New Garden.[33]

Several historians have been misled by Lee's erroneous use of the name of New Garden Meetinghouse. When informed of the location of New Garden Meetinghouse, one historian asked if the meetinghouse on Deep River could have been called New Garden during the time of the Revolutionary War. This was certainly not the case. The Mouzon Map is sufficient proof, but in addition there is a deed to the tract of land on which all of the New Garden Meetinghouses have been built recorded in the Rowan County Courthouse in Salisbury, North Carolina.

New Garden Friends cemetery is visible from the west side of the Guilford College campus. The site of the first meetinghouse is near the center of the present cemetery. That log structure burned in 1784. In 1791 a large frame meetinghouse was erected on the site of the previous building. The area occupied by these meetinghouses is marked clearly. In 1781 the Salisbury Road approached New Garden from the west at approximately the location of Friendly Avenue today and made a sharp turn around New Garden Meetinghouse to the north. From the site of the meetinghouse the ground slopes gently to the south and to the east to what was then the Salisbury Road.

In questioning one of Colonel Lee's interpretations of the Battle of Guilford Courthouse, Judge David Schenck said, "Lee has written so charmingly that his book has become a popular favorite, and, indeed, when he is accurate, no one describes the incidents of the period with more force and beauty than he." [34] After referring to what he considers a major error, Schenck said, ". . . may we not be pardoned for disbelieving the account written by Lee in 1809, twenty–eight years after the battle, from memory alone." [35] As it relates to the Battle of Guilford Courthouse, Lee's error with reference to New Garden Meetinghouse may not be of sufficient importance to mar his credibility, but it is of more importance in the narrative of the Battle of New Garden, especially as it relates to the movement of troops before and after the battle.

APPROACHING THE BATTLE

As indicated earlier, the events leading to the Battle of Guilford Courthouse and to the Battle of New Garden were diverse and geographically widespread. In the month preceding these battles, a wide area of Guilford, Orange, Rockingham, Chatham, and Randolph counties was the arena for numerous maneuvers and counter maneuvers by cavalry and light infantry of the American and British forces. The Battle of New Garden was the last act of this campaign before the Battle of Guilford Courthouse. During the week preceding it, each commander kept his army between the enemy force and his own route for supplies and possible retreat. Cornwallis guarded his route to Cross Creek and Wilmington, and Greene stayed on his road to Virginia. Greene's maneuvers from High Rock Ford, to Troublesome Creek, and on to Guilford Courthouse were all influenced by the location of the British army in relation to the Virginia lifeline of his army.

On March 14th, as noted previously, General Greene moved his army to Guilford Courthouse and in so doing virtually challenged Cornwallis to a long–sought test of strength. Greene knew that the British army was at Deep River Friends Meetinghouse twelve miles away. It had moved to that position from Buffalo Creek, though Lee gives a different interpretation of the British approach to Deep River:

> Feeling his privations daily, Lord Cornwallis, leaving his baggage to follow made a sudden movement late in the evening from Bell's Mill toward New Garden [Deep River], a Quaker settlement abounding in forage and provisions.[36]

Again Lee erroneously attached the name "New Garden" to the Deep River Quaker settlement. He does not tell how or when Cornwallis could have taken his army on the long detour to Bell's Mill during the crowded days prior to the arrival at Deep River. Schenck simplifies the error by putting Bell's Mill near Jamestown in Guilford County, when in reality it is near Randleman in Randolph County, twenty miles from Jamestown. According to Schenck's version, "Cornwallis now withdrew from his camp on the Alamance to Bell's Mill on Deep River not far from where Jamestown now is." [37] One may be tempted to wonder if Judge Schenck did not see Cornwallis moving from what is now the southern part of Greensboro to a point near Jamestown and by mistake applying the name "Bells Mill" to the Mendenhall Mill. One of the sources of Alamance Creek is near South Buffalo Creek, and part of the British army must have been in that area, though a part of it is believed to have been a short distance away on North Buffalo Creek.[38]

It was during the nine days between the Battle of Wetzel's Mill and that of New Garden that Colonel Lee's account would have Cornwallis taking his army on the long detour due south, twenty miles to Bell's Mill, and then to the northeast another twenty or twenty–five miles to Deep River Friends Meetinghouse. A study of the *Order Book* of Cornwallis and of his report to Lord George Germain after the Battle of Guilford Courthouse reveals that the British army did not leave Guilford County during that nine–day period. During that period there was no time in which the army could have made the journey of forty or forty–five miles for even a brief stop at Bell's Mill.

During the first two days after the Battle of Wetzel's Mill, Cornwallis kept his army near the scene of that conflict. On the 9th and

10th of March he made his headquarters at the Gorrell Plantation in the South Buffalo watershed. On the 11th he chose Dillons Mill as his headquarters. On March 12th he was at McGuestions (McCuise).* There Cornwallis issued an order for ". . . the troops to be ready to march at half past 5 o'clock tomorrow morning."[39] When this order was issued Cornwallis was near South Buffalo Creek on the road from New Garden to Pittsboro. In his report to Lord Germain written two days after the Battle of Guilford Courthouse, Cornwallis said, "I had encamped on the 13th instant at the Quaker Meeting between the forks of Deep River."[40]

These documents show that the British army went from the area of South Buffalo Creek to Deep River Meetinghouse and not from Bell's Mill to that place. This does not rule out the possibility that one of the far–ranging foraging parties of the British army was at Bell's Mill on or just before March 12th. If additional evidence is needed, Colonel Tarleton's account may be used. He indicates that after General Greene decided to go to Guilford Courthouse he sent his:

> . . . advanced guards toward a good position above Reedy Fork . . . and pushed forward his light troops to attack the rear of the British as they crossed a branch of Deep River: the legion dragoons repulsed the enemy's detachment with some loss, and the royal army encamped at the Quakers meeting–house.[41]

The British army, moving from either branch of Buffalo Creek to Deep River Meetinghouse, would cross the East Fork of Deep River about one mile from the meetinghouse. It must have been at that point on the Salisbury Road that the attack was made on the rear guard of the British army. Colonel Lee's contradiction of the movement of the British army from Buffalo Creek to Deep River is not convincing. After saying that the British army left Bell's Mill late in the evening on a "sudden movement" toward New Garden (Deep River) he said:

> Some of the small parties of the legion horse traversing in every quarter, one of them approached Bell's Mill and found it abandoned. When informed by the inhabitants that the baggage had lately proceeded under heavy escort the officer commanding the horse determined to trace secretly the progress of its march.[42]

---

* *Lawson calls it M'Cuiston: all are references to same place.*

29

Lee reveals that his cavalry had broken up into small parties and was ranging over wide areas of the countryside, but he lost sight of the main body of the British army. A British foraging party might have left Bell's Mill late in the evening, but it seems very doubtful that the entire British army would have started on a twenty–five mile journey at that time of day. These could have been the supply wagons which Colonel Lee was trying to find and capture when he became lost in the woods near Deep River Meetinghouse. The accounts written by Lord Cornwallis and Benson Lossing show clearly that in the few days prior to March 15th there was no time in which the whole British army could have gone to Bell's Mill. It would have entailed a march of nearly fifty miles and there was no time for it.

The British believed that the Deep River community was a prosperous area and looked forward to obtaining badly needed supplies from the people. In this they were not disappointed. Another asset of the community was Mendenhall's Mill. These are important reasons why Cornwallis moved his army to that location, but a glance at a contemporary map reveals additional reasons. From this place on the Salisbury Road his vital route to Wilmington would be in one direction, and following that road to the northeast would lead him toward the American Army.

After reaching Deep River, the immediate interest of the British commander must have been to find food for the army, for his first order was: "A party of one officer and fifty privates from the Brigade of the Guards to parade immediately and march to Mendenhall's Mill [sic]. A guard will attend from headquarters." [43] On the following day, March 14th, Cornwallis issued a second order which emphasized the importance of the mill to the life of the army:

> The party at Mendenhall's Mill will be relieved at 12 o'clock this day — a sergeant and twelve of which relief will be sent immediately as an escort to the wagons to this mill where they will remain and be joined by the other part of the guard. [44]

The mill had been built by James Mendenhall, who had settled there in the 1750s. His home was on a hill a short distance above the mill. His son, George Mendenhall, had inherited the home and the mill, and his wife, Judith Gardner Mendenhall, and their children lived there during the war. The two orders issued by Cornwallis may verify the tradition that part of the British army camped on a Mendenhall farm, while the major part of the army camped around or near Deep River Meetinghouse.

In writing about her great–grandparents, George and Judith Gardner Mendenhall, Mary Mendenhall Hobbs said:

> A part of Cornwallis' army camped upon the hill near the house, … The British had commandeered the mill and the grain stored there and had also swept the entire premises bare of foodstuff. At last the only remaining milch cow was driven up the hill by the soldiers. There was a houseful of children to be fed and this cow was the only remaining source of supply. Nothing daunted Judith went at once to headquarters of the army and laid the situation before the officer in charge, who at once issued the order that the cow be returned to the owner, Judith walked down the hill leading her cow.[45]

The sight of their mother and their cow parading down the hill to the barn must have given the little Mendenhall children a joyous thrill. Their mother's courage and desperate determination and the sympathy which she had stirred in the heart of the British officer had saved them from the pangs of hunger and their cow from the butcher's knife and the fire of the barbecue pit.

Caruthers preserves a gem of a story (given him by his old friend, Peter Rife) relative to the events in the early hours of the morning of March 15th. The story would have us believe that Colonel Lee, having learned that a British guard had been thrown around the Mendenhall Mill, decided to surprise and capture it:

> On the morning of March 15th Lee was there with his cavalry before daybreak, but the men were all gone. He questioned Mrs. Mendenhall very closely, but all she could tell was that about eleven or twelve o'clock in the night she heard a bugle, apparently at a great distance, but coming very rapidly, still waxing louder as it approached; and five minutes after it arrived they were all gone. Until now it was uncertain that the battle would take place, but this satisfied Lee that the British would be on their way to Martinville at an early hour and he returned to New Garden.[46]

Colonel Lee's *Memoirs* show that he was not at Mendenhall's Mill at the time indicated by the Peter Rife story, but during the night and early morning he was on New Garden Road near Guilford Courthouse. He had sent a Lieutenant Heard to keep watch on the British army camped around Deep River Meetinghouse, and he or some of his men could have enacted the role at the mill which the story attributes to Colonel Lee.

In Tarleton's view, the British at this time were in a desperate situation and had been for several days. In a report made to Lord Germain two days after the Battle of Guilford Courthouse, Cornwallis corroborates Tarleton's evaluation of the situation in which the British army found itself after leaving Hillsborough. In this report he spoke of the "extreme difficulty of subsisting" his army "in the exhausted country." The British commander kept his attention riveted upon his avenue of communication with the British base of supplies on the Cape Fear which he saw "would become indispensably necessary to open." [47] Tarleton reported that Major Craig, who commanded the port of Wilmington, was directed, if he "found it practicable, to transport supplies . . . by water to Cross Creek." However, the presence of a large American force in the area near Cornwallis prevented him from sending any detachment strong enough to guarantee that the supplies would reach the British army in Guilford County.

In Colonel Tarleton's view, this left the British army in serious straits:

> Thus situated, Earl Cornwallis had the alternative, either commence his retreat or prepare for a general action. The power and position of his enemy rendered all the country beyond the pickets hostile to the British cause, which had no friends or partisans at this period except those included within the extent of the royal camp. [48]

In spite of all the obstacles and dangers, Cornwallis did not hesitate to give the order for an advance on Guilford Courthouse as soon as he received the information that Greene had moved his army to that place.

The commanders of the opposing armies sought to provide for every possible contingency, including the possibility of defeat. Cornwallis wrote:

> . . . after detaching Lieutenant Colonel Hamilton with our wagons, and baggage, escorted by his own regiment, a detachment of one hundred infantry and twenty cavalry towards Bell's Mill on Deep River, I marched with the rest of the corps at daybreak on the morning of the 15th, to meet the enemy or attack them in their encampment. [49]

Cornwallis was anxious to get his essential baggage to what he considered a safe place on the route which he would take in the event of defeat. He sent a strong detachment to protect it from any wide–ranging enemy patrol such as Lee's cavalry. If a guess may be permitted, it seems probable that the action reported by Judith Gardner Mendenhall was the removal of provision from the mill to the camp at the meetinghouse to be included in the train of supplies then preparing to start for Bell's Mill.

General Greene was equally anxious to get his valuable baggage to a safe place on the route which he had chosen for a possible retreat. After the Battle of Guilford Courthouse, he wrote to the President of the Continental Congress from his camp at Speedwell Ironworks on Troublesome Creek to which he had retreated: "In this position at the Courthouse we waited the approach of the enemy, having previously sent off the baggage to this place appointed to rendezvous at in case of defeat." [50]

The stage was now set. The two armies were ready, and orders were issued which would lead to sharp fighting on the morning of March 15th. By half past five in the morning, the entire British army was moving out of its camp at Deep River. General Greene had made his plan of battle and had deployed his army on the carefully selected area to the west of Guilford Courthouse along both sides of New Garden Road. At an early hour of the morning he had ordered Colonel Lee, with his Legion and additional infantry, to move out onto New Garden Road to prevent the British from effecting any surprise. Lord Cornwallis ordered Colonel Tarleton to precede the main body of the British army with a strong advance guard. These two forces were destined to meet in an unscheduled battle in the New Garden community.

THE RUNNING BATTLE

The fighting which took place in the morning has been described as a single skirmish so often that a clear picture of its duration, intensity and geographic extent may come as a mild shock to those who are accustomed to such descriptions. General Greene, in his report to the Continental Congress on the day following the battle, emphasized the intensity of the fighting and the heavy casualties, but he too intimated that the morning conflict was only one encounter. He characterized it as a "severe skirmish with Colonel Tarleton, in which the enemy suffered greatly."[51] It is possible that he had not been given a detailed account of the morning conflicts.

Addison Coffin, a local historian of the late nineteenth century, relied on testimony given several decades after the battle by persons who either participated in it, watched part of it, or lived in the area at the time, and so formulated the following characterization of it:

> All historians speak of the engagement near New Garden as a mere skirmish, but in results it was of great importance, and a serious and almost fatal delay to the British advance. Campbell and Lee, with less than 600 riflemen [*sic*], delayed Cornwallis three hours, compelling him to deploy 2,000 men into line of battle to dislodge and drive them from the woods in which they were posted. This enabled Green [*sic*] to perfect his arrangements for the battle at Martinsville.[52]

Here again the magnitude and importance of the battle are made to stand out, but the clear implication is given that the morning conflict was only one encounter. This statement strongly refutes the traditional characterization of the morning battle as a minor skirmish and corroborates the evaluation made by Greene. In stating that it took strong reinforcements to drive the Americans "from the woods in which they were posted," Coffin shows that he must have been thinking of the battle at the Cross Roads.

Cornwallis was another who left the impression that there was only one morning battle:

> About four miles from Guilford our advanced guard commanded by Lieutenant Colonel Tarleton, fell in with a corps of the enemy consisting of Lee's Legion, some back mountain men, and Virginia militia which he attacked with his usual good conduct and spirit and defeated.[53]

This account might place the battle at either New Garden Meetinghouse or at the Cross Roads. In either case, it was the American force which retreated.

In these three accounts the inference is strong that there was only one battle during the morning. One indicates that the conflict lasted for three hours. Three hours is a long time for one skirmish — much longer than the duration of the Battle of Guilford Courthouse.

Only two references have been found which specifically refer to three conflicts in the morning battle. Tradition has Colonel Lee saying that there were three encounters. For this Eli Caruthers relies on the word of Peter Rifle, "a very respectable old gentleman," with whom he had been acquainted for many years and who is reputed to have been in Lee's Legion:

> He said that they had three skirmishes, or bouts as they termed it, three "bouts" with them [the British] before we got to the Court-house and that Lee lost seventeen of his men in the encounters. When they arrived at the scene of action [at Guilford Courthouse], cool as the morning was, their horses were all in a foam of sweat and were nearly broke down; but Col. Lee rode along the front line from one end to the other, exhorting them to stand firm and not be afraid of the British; for he swore that he had whipped them three times that morning, and could do it again.[54]

This assertion that there were three morning battles is corroborated by the Journal of Sergeant Major William Seymour of the Delaware regiment which was in the first line of battle at Guilford Courthouse. In the Seymour account:

> Colonel Lee with his horse and infantry and a detachment of riflemen went to observe their [the British] motion, and meeting with their vanguard, upon which they commenced a smart skirmish, in which Colonel Lee's detachment did wonders, obliging the enemy to give way in three different attacks, driving them into the main army in which they killed and wounded a great number.[55]

Though neither of these informants is equal in prestige to Lord Cornwallis or General Greene, it is possible that they were closer to the morning conflicts than either of the commanders. Much of the information about the fighting during the morning falls into place around the three different conflicts.

When Caruthers said that Lee had ridden twenty–five or thirty miles before the action at Guilford Courthouse, he must have assumed that it was Colonel Lee who scouted Mendenhall Mill on Deep River in the early hours of that morning. Though Lee was on New Garden Road at that time, the hard riding and sharp fighting in which he was engaged between sunrise and noon were enough to tire both horse and rider.

Through the night of March 14th, Colonel Lee kept Lieutenant Heard, with a contingent of mounted troops, probing the picket lines around the British camp at Deep River Meetinghouse. Their only listening device was the human ear, and, since the British pickets kept Heard's men at a considerable distance from their camp, the American interpretation of what was going on in or near the camp was subject to error. It is not surprising that Lieutenant Heard was deceived by the rumble of the moving wagons and the trample of horses of the escorting cavalry as they moved out of the British camp to begin the journey to Bell's Mill. Heard sent a message to the American camp that the British were moving out on the Salisbury Road in the middle of the night to begin the march toward Guilford Courthouse. Colonel Lee records the reaction in the American camp:

> About two in the morning this officer [Lieutenant Heard] communicated that a large body of horse were approaching ... Lee was directed to advance with his cavalry... the van was called at four in the morning to take breakfast with all practicable haste. This had just been finished when the last mentioned order from the general was communicated. Lieutenant Colonel Lee instantly mounted, and took to the enemy, at the head of the horse.[56]

Actually the British did not begin their march toward Guilford Courthouse until 5:30 in the morning, after Colonel Lee had started his force out on New Garden Road. The principal effect of Heard's premature alarm was to get Lee's men through an early breakfast in preparation for the hard day ahead. The British soldiers were forced to march and fight through the whole day without any food.

As the British army moved along the Salisbury Road from Deep River to New Garden, the American pickets under Lieutenant Heard were pushed well ahead of the advance guard of the British army. Where the Salisbury Road makes a sharp turn around New Garden Meetinghouse, the pickets of the two hostile armies elected to fire a volley at one another. Colonel Tarleton's account of this beginning of the day's conflict gives the distance of the event from Deep River Meetinghouse, and this lends some support to the tradition that the first exchange of shots of the day took place at New Garden Meetinghouse: "The British had proceeded seven miles on the Great Salisbury Road to Guilford when the light troops drove in a picket of enemy." [57] There is no evidence that anyone was injured, and the incident would be considered unimportant if it had not been the herald of the most significant day of fighting in the entire Revolutionary War in North Carolina. After this incident Lieutenant Heard retreated slowly, followed by Tarleton's Cavalry until they met Colonel Lee's cavalry at some point on New Garden Road north of the Cross Roads. This set the stage for the first of the three important encounters in the Battle of New Garden.

THE CLASH IN THE LANE

Colonel Lee left Deep River on March 14th to rejoin the main army. When he found General Greene and the American army at Guilford Courthouse he was ". . . immediately advanced on the road towards the quaker meeting–house [New Garden] with orders to post himself within two or three miles of the court house." [58] It is presumed that Lee's force camped at the assigned place on the night of March 14th, and it must have been from this point that he began his advance toward the approaching British army early the next morning, in compliance with General Greene's order. In this, the first American action of the day, "the cavalry had not proceeded above two miles when Lee was met by Lieutenant Heard and his party who were retiring followed leisurely by the enemy horse." [59] In the light of the two references to distance given above, Colonel Lee could have met Lieutenant Heard a short distance northeast of the Cross Roads. Wherever they were, the American colonel effected an orderly retreat to a position which he considered suitable for a clash with the enemy cavalry. He indicated that this retrograde movement was to enable him to take a position nearer the main army and closer to the approaching "rifle militia" of his command.

Colonel Tarleton mistook this movement for the beginning of a hasty retreat to the main army at the Courthouse. Lee retreated to a position on New Garden Road which was in a long lane with high rail fences on both sides of the road. It was a most unlikely place for a cavalry battle, but Lee had his reason for choosing it. When Tarleton ordered a charge it could only strike a few Americans in the front ranks. The assault had little effect on the Americans. The second had the same result. At this time, Lee was with Captain Armstrong and his company of cavalry. Of the battle, Lee had this to say:

> At this moment, Lee ordering a charge, the dragoons came instantly to a right about, and, in close column, rushed upon the foe. The meeting happened in a long lane, with high curved fences on either side of the road. . . . The charge was ordered by Lee, from conviction that he should trample his enemy under foot if he dared to meet the shock . . . . Tarleton sounding a retreat . . . the whole of the enemy's [front] section was dismounted [unhorsed] and many of the horses prostrated, some of the dragoons killed, the rest made prisoners [those thrown from their horses]: not a single American soldier or horse was injured. Tarleton retired with celerity.[60]

This was Lee's version of the cavalry battle in the Lane. The claim made by Cornwallis in his report to Lord Germain that Colonel Tarleton won the battle certainly must have referred to the whole morning battle rather than to the encounter in the Lane.

If Lee lured Tarleton to attack in this unlikely place it must have been because he believed his men and their mounts were superior to their adversaries. If he avoided a battle in the open because he believed the British cavalry numerically superior he did not know that twenty of Tarleton's men had been sent to Bell's Mill to protect the baggage train.

If Lee's description of the encounter in the Lane is correct, his trap proved to be a success. After Tarleton had sent two charges against Lee's position without success, Lee ordered a countercharge. The front segment of the opposing cavalry was given a severe shock. Men were knocked from their horses, some were killed, others captured. Lee said his men suffered no casualties.

Tarleton was quick to see his disadvantage and immediately ordered a retreat, terminating the battle with a different result from that indicated by Cornwallis. This was strictly a cavalry battle. The infantry which had been assigned to Colonel Lee's force must have been approaching the scene of the battle and would soon have been ready to support the cavalry if it had been needed. The infantry of the British advance guard was too far away to give Colonel Tarleton any hope of assistance.

In searching for the exact location of the Battle in the Lane, only faint clues give any basis for conjecture. One of these is the distance from the point from which Colonel Lee started his advance that morning. The other is the assertion that the battle took place in a segment of the New Garden Road which was ". . . a long lane with big curved fences on either side of the road. . . ." In that day the law of North Carolina permitted people to let their horses, cattle, hogs, and other livestock range freely over the countryside, regardless of the owner-ship of the land. This forced farmers to build fences around their fields to prevent the free–ranging domestic animals from destroying their crops. Since this segment of the road was in a "long lane," the fields on either side of the road must have been large. The only place along New Garden Road near the point in distance indicated above, where the terrain would be suitable for large fields on both sides of the road, is near the entrance to the present Jefferson Standard Country Club.* The distance of Lee's camp from the Courthouse and the distance he travelled to meet Lieutenant Heard support this conjecture. No evi-dence has been found in the area, or in tradition, of the graves of the men killed in this encounter.

AROUND NEW GARDEN MEETINGHOUSE

In fleeing from the clash with the American cavalry, Colonel Tarleton led his cavalry onto a road branching southeast from New Garden Road. The route chosen must have been a narrow one through a wooded area, across what is now the campus of Guilford College.[61] After proceeding for approximately one–half mile to the road from Buffalo Creek, Tarleton was able to turn right and reach New Garden Meetinghouse and the Salisbury Road on which the main body of the British army was approaching.

Instead of following Tarleton on this detour, Colonel Lee quickly devised a plan to cut him off from the main body of the British army and destroy or capture his force:

> . . . being well acquainted with the county, he followed the common route by the quaker meeting–house, with a view to sever the British

---

*　*Reprint editor's note: see footnote, p. 17.*

39

lieutenant colonel from his army by holding him well upon his [Lee's] left . . . and thus place his horse [Lee's cavalry] between Tarleton and Cornwallis, presumed to be some distance behind.[62]

It was a simple, well–laid plan. Upon reaching the road intersection at New Garden Meetinghouse, Lee's superior cavalry would stand between Tarleton's cavalry on their left and the British army approaching on their right — hopefully some distance away. In this maneuver the eager American colonel ran into a surprise. At the road intersection by the meetinghouse, his cavalry charged head–on into the infantry of the approaching advance guard of the British army. In the words of the surprised Colonel Lee, "As Lee, with his column in full speed, got up to the meeting–house, the British guards had just reached it; displaying in a moment, gave the American cavalry a close general fire." [63] The British infantry of the advance guard arrived at the intersection just in time to give Lee an unexpected shock and spoil his design on the cavalry of Colonel Tarleton.

Soon after the initial clash, reinforcements arrived for both sides, and the nature of the battle changed. Tarleton's cavalry must have reached the scene soon after the first clash. This put Lee at a disadvantage, and he ordered a retreat. This order was immediately countermanded when Lee's

> Legion infantry came running up with trailed arms, and opened a well aimed fire on the [British] guards, which was followed in a few minutes by a volley from the riflemen under Campbell, who had taken post on the left of the infantry. The action became sharp and was bravely maintained on both sides.[64]

This short statement indicates that the two infantry forces in Colonel Lee's command had arrived and taken their places in the line of battle in the grove around New Garden Meetinghouse. It may be assumed that the full complements of cavalry and infantry of the advance guard of the two armies, numbering possibly more than a thousand men, were now battling one another on Quaker grounds. Numerically the two forces were about evenly matched. There can be little doubt that, when "[t]he action became sharp and was bravely maintained on both sides," [65] there were many charges and counterattacks on the gentle slope around New Garden Meetinghouse. Certainly this log meetinghouse provided protective cover for some of the

American riflemen firing at their enemies around corners, through windows and doors and through holes which they were able to make in the chinking between logs in the walls.

Colonel Lee attempts to give the time of the beginning of the battle in recording that "[i]t was now about one hour after sunrise . . . [and] the sun had risen just above the trees." [66] At that time of year, this would have placed the beginning of the battle at 7:15. In view of all that had taken place since 5:30 that morning when the British left their camp, Lee's memory of the time of the onset of the encounter may be questioned.

The conflict around New Garden Meetinghouse lasted for thirty or forty minutes — sufficient time for much to take place which may not have been recorded in the meager accounts of the fighting. References to the heavy casualties, including the deaths of several officers of the two forces, indicate that this was more than a light clash.[67] The wound which Banastre Tarleton received was not fatal, but it has received more attention than some of the fatalities. His right hand was shattered by a musketball, causing him to lose his middle and index fingers.[68] During the remainder of the day he rode with his hand bandaged and his arm in a sling. This was no doubt a painful and debilitating experience.

In the type of warfare which Lee and Tarleton were waging, it was just as important to know when to retreat as when to order an advance. As noted, when Lee's men seemed to be outnumbered early in the affray at the meetinghouse, the American colonel ordered a retreat. This order was countermanded when Lee's two infantry forces arrived on the run. After thirty or forty minutes of hard fighting, possibly on fairly equal terms with heavy casualties on both sides:

> [t]he cavalry having formed again in a column and Lee being convinced, from the appearance of the guards, that Cornwallis was not far in the rear, drew off his infantry; and covering them from any attempt of the British horse retired towards the American army.[69]

This description of the retreat indicates that it was prompted by the belief that the main body of the British army was approaching and not by any superiority of the British force engaged in the combat. It was an orderly withdrawal with the cavalry protecting the infantry from the pursuing British until it reached its new position at the Cross Roads.

No reliable account of the number of dead and wounded resulting from the battle around the meetinghouse has been found. Levi Coffin has written: "A number of soldiers were killed near the meetinghouse and along the road, and were buried by the roadside and in the Friends burying ground near the meetinghouse. I have often seen their graves." [70] Evidence of these graves has long since disappeared.[71]

Additional information is given by Lee:

> The British sustained a much heavier loss in killed and wounded than we did. His fire was innocent, overshooting the cavalry entirely: whose caps and accoutrements were all struck with green twigs, cut by British ball out of large oaks in the meetinghouse yard, under which the cavalry received the volley of the guards. Some of the infantry and riflemen were killed, and more wounded: among them was lieutenant Snowden, of the legion infantry, who with most of the wounded was necessarily left on the field.[72]

The American dead and most of the wounded were left on the ground around the meetinghouse. Captain James Tate of the American Legion was mortally wounded and died there. He was buried in the New Garden cemetery near the meetinghouse.[73] Lieutenant Snowden died of his wounds and must have been buried in or near that cemetery.[74] Most of the British dead and seriously wounded were lying in or near the road. Lieutenant Ernst von Trott of the Bose regiment was mortally wounded.[75]

These grim scenes around New Garden Meetinghouse during and after the battle offered a sharp contrast to what took place on the same grounds on "First–days" and "Fourth–days," when local Friends hitched their horses under these same trees and went quietly into the meetinghouse for silent worship.

As the two forces left the meetinghouse grounds and moved toward the Cross Roads fighting each other all the way, their dead and seriously wounded were left where they fell. In this way the battle around New Garden Meetinghouse came to an end.

It is seven tenths of a mile from the meetinghouse to the Cross Roads. Except for a small field near the Cross Roads, the road was through a wooded area poorly suited for the use of the cavalry. However, the American cavalry covered the retreat of the infantry and gave Lee's force sufficient time to take a strong position in the woods at the Cross Roads.

AT THE CROSS ROADS

The Hessians kept up a continuous attack on Colonel Lee's forces during their withdrawal from the meetinghouse, suffering some casualties. The mortally wounded were buried where they fell in graves which were visible more than fifty years later. Tradition pictures some of the New Garden Boarding School pupils, armed with picks and shovels, playing the role of archaeologists attempting to determine whether the low mounds along the road were actually graves. When they struck human skeletons, they hastily refilled the graves and left them for time to remove all evidence of their location.[76]

Another tradition preserved by Addison Coffin describes an incident which took place near the beginning of the battle. It also gives a glimpse of the terrain, including a small field, which the British had to cross in front of the woods in which the Americans had taken their position:

> There was a large log house near the southeast of the spring, . . . In 1781 a man, named Hunt, lived in the same log house. On the morning of the Guilford battle, a 16 year old son of Hunt, was hid in some bushes on the line fence between the College[77] and John Ballinger's land to see the battle at the Cross Roads. While excitedly looking and listening, the British Light Horse suddenly came into the field on the College s[i]de of the fence out of the wood. The captain sounded a charge on his bugle with the intent of a flank movement. On the impulse of the moment young Hunt leveled his "smoothbore" gun and fired. The captain fell dead. The cavalry supposing the fence lined with sharpshooters, turned and fled.[78]

Colonel Tarleton said of the encounter at the Cross Roads, "Captain Goodrick of the guards, a promising young officer, fell in this contest and between twenty and thirty of the guards, dragoons, and yagers were killed and wounded." [79] A comparison of the two accounts produces some ground for the assumption that Captain Goodrick was killed by the Hunt teenager who was concealed behind the fence, waiting for a view of the battle.

The battle at the Cross Roads was the heaviest engagement of the morning. Certainly more men were engaged here than in either of the other clashes. The British force was comprised of Colonel Tarleton's cavalry and infantry, the Bose regiment, the Yagers and the Twenty–third Regiment of Webster's Brigade, which arrived after the battle had been in progress for a short time. The American side included Colonel Lee's Legion of both cavalry and infantry and Campbell's riflemen from the mountains of Virginia and North Carolina, including those under Colonel Preston. It is assumed that Captain Armstrong's company was with Colonel Lee throughout the morning.

When the Twenty–third Regiment arrived, the British must have become numerically superior. As noted above, Addison Coffin's account of the battle has Cornwallis throwing about four–fifths of his entire army against Lee's well placed force. He based his interpretation on what he considered strong contemporary evidence:

> This skirmish or battle was witnessed by John and Rebecca Ballinger, and participated in by Samuel Lamb, from whom I received much of my information. Also, those who assisted in burying the dead that and the next day, testified to the fact that this was a real battle and a serious loss on both sides.[80]

From these contemporaries of the battle, he was led to believe that Cornwallis found it necessary to bring two thousand men or four–fifths of his army into the conflict before Lee was forced to relinquish his strong position and leave the way open for the British army to move on to Guilford Courthouse. Even though this account of the size of the force used by the British to dislodge the Americans has not been corroborated, there is reason for giving it serious consideration. Only a short time before this, Colonel Lee had ordered a retreat from the meetinghouse because he was convinced that the main body of the British army was approaching on the road from Deep River. At the Cross Roads the Americans had delayed their withdrawal and held their position against Colonel Tarleton's force. It is quite possible that sufficient time had elapsed for the main body of the British army to reach the Cross Roads. The terrain in front of the American position was favorable to the use of a large number of men in the British attack.

For Cornwallis it may have been a case of using the troops as they arrived in the course of their march toward Guilford Courthouse rather than ordering up reinforcements. The British commander would certainly have used his advancing forces as they were needed to clear the way for movement toward General Greene's position at the Courthouse. In light of this view of the situation, Coffin's story seems plausible. However, a British account of the battle does not corroborate the Coffin story:

> Lee behaved with great bravery, and maintained his ground with firmness, until the appearance of the twenty–third regiment, advancing to support Tarleton, obliged the Americans to retire with precipitation.[81]

It is possible that Lord Cornwallis was at the Cross Roads in person before the end of the battle and with him some of his main subordinates: Colonel James Webster, General Alexander Leslie, and General Charles O'Hara.

Whatever the strength of the British force in this encounter, the Americans must have repulsed a series of assaults. The battle lasted for approximately one–half hour. Since crippling the enemy was the primary objective of both sides, each commander claimed the victory and asserted that the enemy had suffered the greater number of casualties. The number of troops involved gives some support to tradition's report of the heavy casualties. The dead were buried in a little graveyard of twenty or more graves which were visible until around 1900. This cemetery was located on the rim of a cove which was behind the American position.

In the late 1930s, Delos Ballinger, whose home on Ballinger Road may be seen from the Cross Roads, told me that down to within his lifetime some of his relatives received money from an English family to pay for the upkeep of some of the graves in the little cemetery. For some reason the payments stopped, the graves were neglected, and in time all evidence of their existence eroded away. No one knows if more than one soldier was buried in any of the graves, as was done in some instances at New Garden.

The large log house which stood on the rim of the cove near the graveyard was a landmark at the time of the battle and became important as a hospital in which British and American soldiers wounded at the Cross Roads were treated.[82]

The retreat of the Americans from the Cross Roads ended the Battle of New Garden. Colonel Lee effected a rapid but seemingly orderly retreat to the position assigned to his men in the front line at Guilford Courthouse. It is not possible to determine with certainty the exact time of the end of the battle. A study of the available evidence leaves the impression that the retreat from the Cross Roads began before eleven o'clock, and the British arrived in sight of the first line of the Americans at noon. The attack on the first line began, then, about one o'clock in the afternoon.

THE BATTLE OF GUILFORD COURTHOUSE

The history of the Battle of Guilford Courthouse has been given more attention in the histories of the state and in histories of the Revolutionary War in North Carolina than any other battle fought on North Carolina soil. In some of these, the story has been given in considerable detail. For this reason, its treatment in this treatise is restricted to its relation to the Battle of New Garden and its influence on the Quakers in this area.

The battle lasted for approximately two hours, with heavy casualties on both sides. General Greene withdrew his army from the battle and left the field to the British. Though the British had suffered greater casualties than the Americans, General Greene decided to save his army from the possibility of serious damage for a later battle with the British. He led his army to the prearranged place of rendezvous at the Speedwell Ironworks on Troublesome Creek. There he reassembled his force and waited for the attack which never came.

Cornwallis had lost one fourth of his army through casualties. Ammunition and medical supplies had been reduced to a dangerous level, and a lack of adequate clothing and other supplies left the army in great need. The British were in no position to attack the Americans at Speedwell Ironworks. The one alternative left to Cornwallis was to hasten to some place where his army could be rehabilitated. He had won the Battle of Guilford Courthouse, but he had lost the campaign for the control of North Carolina. Three days after the battle, he left

Guilford Courthouse to begin the long march to Wilmington. Two days later Greene came back to Guilford Courthouse before starting in pursuit of Cornwallis.

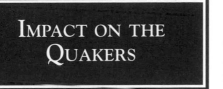

In attempting to evaluate the impact of the war on the Quakers in Guilford and adjoining counties, it is necessary to trace the courses of the opposing armies as they marched through Quaker communities in their maneuvers before and after the Battle of Guilford Courthouse. Although General Greene soon learned the direction taken by Cornwallis on his retreat from Guilford Courthouse, he could not be certain of his ultimate destination, be it Wilmington by way of Cross Creek or Virginia by way of Hillsborough. When Greene began the pursuit of the British he did not follow their trail. He chose instead a course which would enable him to keep within striking distance of the enemy no matter which destination Cornwallis might select.

The British army left Guilford Courthouse via the Salisbury Road and passed through the New Garden community. This was the shortest route to Bell's Mill and Cross Creek. Having left Guilford Courthouse about ten o'clock on the morning of March 18th, the army must have reached New Garden about noon. Again it is necessary to question an account by Colonel Lee, when he says that Cornwallis "...put his army in motion for New Garden where his rear guard with his baggage met him." [83] The implication is that the army stopped at New Garden for the night, and the British supply wagons, which had been sent to Bell's Mill before the Battle of Guilford Courthouse, met the army there. Without doubt this is another of Lee's errors about the location of New Garden Meetinghouse. It would be difficult to imagine that Cornwallis would have his army stop at New Garden for the night, only four and one–half miles from the Courthouse. Deep River Meetinghouse, on the other hand, was twelve miles away — a fair distance to march after a late start. Since they had camped there for two days before the Battle of Guilford Courthouse, this would be familiar ground to the British and Mendenhall Mill was conveniently near.

A statement by Colonel Tarleton may support the belief that the

British army camped for a night at Deep River rather than at New Garden. "Earl Cornwallis therefore began his march on the 18th for Deep River, on his way to Cross Creek." [84] While this reference could be to the Deep River Valley instead of to the meetinghouse by that name, the meetinghouse was in the valley and on the Salisbury Road. An order written by Cornwallis at ten o'clock on the night of March 18th shows that the headquarters of the British commander were at "Ticino's Plantation." [85] This could have been a farm near Deep River Meetinghouse, although nothing has been found to verify it.

The British reached Bell's Mill on the nineteenth, where they rested and foraged for two days. Upon leaving Bell's Mill, Cornwallis left the direct road to Cross Creek and led his army eastward to Cane Creek Meetinghouse near Simon Dixon's Mill. Colonel Tarleton indicates that this maneuver was not to confuse General Greene, for Cornwallis knew that the American army had already crossed Buffalo Creek on the direct road to Cane Creek; rather, it was "to move through a country well supplied with forage." [86] Tradition indicates that they were not disappointed. They took from the farmers in this Quaker community a large number of cattle and sheep and butchered them on the meetinghouse grounds. By robbing them of their grain and live-stock, the British left their imprint on the minds of the Quakers in the Cane Creek community. Unwittingly they left a name for the community. A well–known tradition says a snow storm covered the country-side and caused the British camp to be called "Snow Camp" — a name which settled on the community as a permanent label.

As recorded by Colonel Tarleton, General Greene pursued the British army via a road which crossed the South Buffalo Creek watershed. It must have been the road which at that time followed a direct course to Cane Creek Meetinghouse. To reach this road, Greene had a choice of two roads as he was leaving Guilford Courthouse. One of these was the Salisbury Road to New Garden and the other was the New Salisbury Road. The American troops could have used either or both of these to reach the road across the South Buffalo Creek area. There is a tradition that General Greene stopped at New Garden to talk with Friends about their care of wounded soldiers.

Somewhere south of Buffalo Creek General Greene halted his army for two days to attend to a deficiency in his military supplies. Except for this delay, he might have been able to overtake Cornwallis at Cane Creek Meetinghouse.

From Cane Creek Meetinghouse the British army followed a road downstream to an intersection with the Hillsborough–Wilmington Road at Lindley's Mill. Here Cornwallis turned south toward Pittsboro and Ramsey's Mill and removed all doubt that his destination was Wilmington. General Greene used the same roads in his pursuit of Cornwallis from Cane Creek to Ramsey's Mill.[87]

Friends in the New Garden community had felt the sting of war before the battles exploded in their midst. For several weeks prior to the battles they had been victims of foragers from both armies. The impression is given that all of the farms in the area were hit by this scouring of the country for supplies. Nathan Hunt, a young married man, lived on New Garden Road. His farm was a target for foragers. His food supplies and his livestock were taken. One party took his horses, and another took his milch cow. The raids left Nathan and Martha Hunt and their children almost destitute.[88] Elijah Coffin, reared on a farm near that of Nathan Hunt, said, ". . . the citizens of that part of the country felt in various ways the cruelty and horrors of such a conflict." [89] The struggle between the Whigs and Tories for the control of the government of North Carolina resulted in a breakdown of law and governmental authority, followed by a rash of all sorts of crimes. Robbers, pretending to be soldiers, came to the Coffin home in the middle of the night, threatened the life of William Coffin, and then procceded to rob one of his neighbors. At another time, soldiers came to the Coffin home and took clothing from the family. Later, Elijah Coffin continued, ". . . my dear father ever looked upon his preservation and protection as a kind of interposition of Divine Providence." Everybody in the community suffered.

During the actual battle of New Garden, forces maneuvered and fought through the heart of the settlement. New Garden Meetinghouse and much of the Quaker community were in the center of the struggle. One Quaker said of the day of bloodshed, "It has been uniformly spoken of as a day of great solemnity and awfulness." [90]

A TEST OF QUAKER FAITH

During the Revolutionary War Quakers were put to a severe test as they stood by their widely known testimony that war is evil and that supporting it in any way is contrary to the Christian way of life. In 1777 the North Carolina Yearly Meeting of Friends warned its members against taking the oath or affirmation of allegiance required by the state, as this would signify supporting one of the warring parties. A year later the Yearly Meeting recommended that Friends who made this pledge of allegiance should be disowned. Some members of the Society disregarded the principles of their faith and either joined one of the military forces or made the pledge of allegiance. They were promptly disowned by their local meetings. These deviations from Quakerism, as they applied to war, made the Society of Friends more vulnerable to the barbs which have been thrown by tradition at this aspect of their faith. New Garden Friends have not been immune to these darts. There is a story of one member of this meeting whose farm in the Buffalo Creek area had been swept clean of grain, cattle, and horses by British foragers. He joined Greene's army at Guilford Courthouse for the day of the battle. When he left home early that morning, as the story goes, he told his wife that he was going on a day's hunt, and she provided food for the day. When he returned late in the evening empty handed, his wife asked: "Didn't thee kill any game?" His reply was: "Nothing worth bringing home." One weakness in this tradition is that the man named in the story did not join New Garden Meeting until after the battle.

In the story of the sixteen–year–old son of a Hunt family who killed the British captain near the Cross Roads, the implication is strong that he was a Quaker. The story was recorded by Addison Coffin, a prominent Quaker who lived near the scene of the battle and must have known members of the family. Since the boy's given name does not appear in the story, it is not possible to check the records of New Garden Meeting for his name. However, the New Garden Minutes do not show that any one by the name of Hunt was disowned during the period of the Revolutionary War for "appearing in a warlike manner."

Tradition also carried the story that as many as three hundred men from a wide area around Guilford Courthouse volunteered their services to the American army, fought through the Battle at the Courthouse, and returned home that evening. If this is true, it would be no surprise were some of these men from Quaker families.

The Minutes of New Garden Meeting for July 27, 1781 show that a John Wright was complained of "for taking up arms in a warlike

50

manner." One month later he was disowned for that offense. The dates indicate that he could have been in the battle at the Courthouse. Before the battle, New Garden Meeting disowned four men for "appearing in a warlike manner." On December 25, 1779, this Meeting disowned eleven members for "taking an affirmation of fidelity to the present powers." [91] These actions give clear indication that New Garden Meeting stood firmly by the Quaker belief that war is evil and that Friends should not support it in any way. Deep River Monthly Meeting disowned members for these same reasons.

General Nathanael Greene is called "The Quaker" in a well–known treatise on the Revolutionary War in the South.[92] His father had been a Quaker minister, and he had been a member of a Friends meeting in Rhode Island. He was disowned by his meeting in 1775 for participating in military drills.

Colonel Charles Lynch, who commanded a regiment of Virginia riflemen in the front line in the Battle of Guilford Courthouse, had been a member of the Society of Friends before the war. He and his wife, Anne Terrell Lynch, had taken a leading part in the founding of the town of Lynchburg and in setting up the Quaker meeting at that frontier settlement. The meeting which he had helped to found did not hesitate to disown him when he disregarded Quaker principles by taking up arms. After the war he is said to have attended Quaker meetings for worship, but he never asked to be reinstated as a member.[93]

Peter Rifle, who is mentioned several times by Caruthers in his *Revolutionary Incidents* as a member of Lee's Legion, is said to have been a member of the Society of Friends. No proof of his membership has been found.

BURYING THE DEAD AND CARING FOR THE WOUNDED

As the Battle of New Garden shifted from one place to another the two contending military forces left their dead and seriously wounded lying where they fell. The grounds around New Garden Meetinghouse and at the Cross Roads must have been grim pictures after the fighting ended and the two forces had moved on to the next scene of conflict. Many dead and seriously wounded were scattered over these grounds. The responsibility for them was left to the conscience of the people who lived nearby. That afternoon and the following day men worked at the task of burying the dead. It is known that the casualties were heavy, but the number of the dead and seriously wounded is still a matter of speculation. In 1830 people who had:

> . . . taken part in the battle or in burying the dead and caring for the wounded pointed out mounds in the burial ground at New Garden that contained 21 bodies of the wounded who died in the old meetinghouse, from the battle near by, and the pit near Tate's grave, in the woods, had 20 of the dead buried in it, while the Hessians were buried in the open field where they fell, like animals.[94]

This account was written in 1892. At that time other graves of soldiers who died from wounds received in the Battle of Guilford Courthouse were also visible. Cornwallis had sent seventy–one mortally wounded British soldiers and an undisclosed number of seriously wounded Americans to New Garden for the care of Friends. These soldiers were buried in long trenches in the grave yard. The graves could still be seen in 1892. This brings the total to at least 112 buried in or near New Garden cemetery. This figure is not complete, as the number of Americans brought there by Cornwallis who died of their wounds is not known — nor is the number of seriously wounded British and Americans who died in the homes of New Garden Friends. They must have been buried in the New Garden graveyard. A conservative estimate of the number of soldiers buried in or near this cemetery would place the total between 125 and 150.

During the past twenty–five years, gravediggers have found parts of human skeletons while digging graves in the New Garden cemetery. Two of these were near the east border of the present graveyard, and one was on the gently sloping hillside above the northwest corner of the cemetery.[95] These parts of the present cemetery were in the woods adjoining the graveyard in 1781.

Burying the dead was hard work, but it was accomplished in a short time. The care of the wounded was a prolonged task requiring patient labor day and night. In some cases it must have lasted for several weeks. The number of wounded soldiers cared for by New Garden Friends can be approached only from descriptive bits of information from scattered sources. That forty or fifty were wounded in all the conflicts of the Battle of New Garden does not seem to be a reckless estimate. Of these the seriously wounded must have been cared for in local homes.

As noted, in addition to those wounded in the Battle of New Garden, the care of a large number of the fatally wounded from the Battle of Guilford Courthouse was thrust upon these Friends. Colonel Tarleton said that two days after the Battle Lord Cornwallis sent to New Garden wounded British soldiers ". . .to the amount of seventy with several Americans who were in the same situation. . . lodged under a flag of truce, in the New Garden meeting–house and adjacent buildings." [96] On the following day, March 18th, the British army left Guilford Courthouse to begin the long journey to Wilmington. A large number of wounded men went with the army, but:

> Sixty–four of the wounded, the "bad cases," had to be left behind. Cornwallis left them at the Quaker meeting–house in New Garden, under the care of the surgeon, Mr. Hill and two surgeon mates.[97]

No corroborating source has been found for this second category of wounded left at New Garden. It is the only reference to the British having left behind any surgical or medical assistance for the wounded. If this can be relied upon, 134 wounded British soldiers and an undisclosed number of Americans were left to the mercy and care of New Garden Friends by the Lord Cornwallis. Add to these the unknown number of American and British soldiers seriously wounded in the Battle of New Garden and the Battle at the Cross Roads; the total number must have been between 170 and 190. This is not the end of the story of the humanitarian efforts of New Garden Friends to relieve the suffering which came out of the battles between the British and the Americans on March 15th, however.

On March 20th, General Greene wrote General Daniel Morgan from Guilford Courthouse, to which he had just returned after reorganizing his army at the Speedwell Ironworks on Troublesome Creek: "The enemy are now retiring from us and have left us one hundred and seventy or eighty of their wounded." [98] Cornwallis had left these at Guilford Courthouse two days before when he began his withdrawal to Wilmington. He might have justified this action as one of the exigencies of war. Greene was eager to start in pursuit of his adversary, and he in turn abandoned the wounded American and British soldiers to the conscience and care of the people of the area. In the words of his biographer, "Having received his supplies Greene immediately pursued the enemy, leaving behind him, all the wounded of the British army, that had fallen in his possession and such of his own who were unfit to be removed." [99] No indication has been found of the number "of his own" who were left behind. Certainly the number must have been sufficient to bring the total to more than 250. Since there was no third army to receive them, this burden was left to the people in the area, with a special appeal to the Quakers for their care. After leaving Guilford Courthouse, Nathanael Greene is reported to have stopped at New Garden to urge Quakers to do what they could for these unfortunate men. Nearly a week later he made a second strong appeal by letter. In their reply New Garden Friends reminded Greene that they were already carrying a very heavy burden in the care of the wounded, that at that time they were caring for approximately one hundred in their meetinghouse, but they would do all they could for the wounded at the Courthouse. There was certainly not enough floorspace in the old meetinghouse to accommodate one hundred wounded men. This makes it apparent that there may have been tents or other forms of temporary shelter to care for the overflow. Tarleton referred to the wounded being cared for in "adjacent buildings." * The letter to Greene made no reference to the great number of wounded Americans and British who were cared for in the homes in this community. All of these references and estimates, whatever the exact numbers, add up to a tremendous humanitarian effort on the part of New Garden Friends.

In the nursing duties at the meetinghouse, the men must have been the main force, but in the homes the women undoubtedly carried as much of the load as the men, if not more. History permits few glimpses into New Garden homes as they were filling the role of hospital wards. The two–story log house which stood near the Cross Roads has been referred to as a hospital for the wounded and is reputed to have been filled with casualties from the battle at that place. The number of men treated in this house is not known. Caring for the wounded in the homes was done at great risk to members of families, for some of the wounded men brought the dreaded plague of smallpox with them.

Levi Coffin gives an illuminating view into two homes located on New Garden Road:

---

* *See note no. 96.*

After the battle the meeting–house was used as a hospital for the wounded soldiers, and my grandfather Williams's house was occupied by wounded British officers. My grandfather Coffin's house was used by American officers as a hospital for their sick and wounded. The two farms joined, and the headquarters of the different forces were thus in close proximity.

The smallpox broke out among the British officers and my grandfather Williams caught the disease from them and died. My grandmother was left with twelve children, five sons and seven daughters.[100]

Levi Coffin's grandparents were Richard and Prudence (Beals) Williams and William and Priscilla (Paddock) Coffin.

It is a pity that the number of patients in each of these homes was not given. In view of the tragedy resulting from the Williams family's taking wounded officers who were the carriers of smallpox, one can only wonder if, among the "sick and wounded" who were cared for in the Coffin home, there were not also some who had the disease.

At the time of the battle, Nathan Hunt was twenty–one years old and a member of New Garden Meeting. He was married and had two small children. He volunteered to do nursing duty at the meetinghouse where some among the wounded were being treated for smallpox. Nathan knew that his father, William Hunt, and his cousin, John Woolman, had both died of smallpox while on religious visits in England. Fully conscious of this, and in the face of the opposition of members of his own family, Nathan still felt it his duty to risk his own life to save the lives of these unfortunate men. He contracted the disease, but it proved to be a light case, and he recovered.[101]

These instances give clear evidence that Quakers made no distinction between friends and so–called enemies in their efforts to bind up the wounds left by war. Here also is evidence that New Garden Friends put the call of religious faith above their own lives. Richard Williams and Nathan Hunt went voluntarily into danger's midst. One lost his life; the other survived. The members of these families must not have been alone. Others also came in harm's way, and the story is not complete until we see the women and the children sharing danger as bravely as the men. Prudence Williams, Martha Hunt, and Priscilla Coffin have been recognized among this company, and there must have been many more.

LESS SERIOUS CASUALTIES

There were many less serious casualties from the battle around New Garden Meetinghouse. One of these was Colonel Banastre Tarleton. "A musketball shattered the first and middle fingers of his right hand." [102] During the remainder of the day he rode in all the battles in which his men were engaged with his right hand bandaged and his arm in a sling, unable to use a weapon of any kind. Who bandaged his hand? Elijah Coffin wrote into the family remembrances of that fateful day:

> During the progress of the battle, a soldier came in great haste to my mother at the dwelling, having two fingers shot off and bleeding, which she kindly dressed for him as well as she could and he hastened back to the conflict. [103]

Was it the right hand? Could two soldiers have had two fingers shot off one hand in the morning battle? Or, was this "Bloody Tarleton?" He certainly would have come in haste and would have hurried back to his command.

This must have presented a rare picture. Here was Hannah Dicks Coffin, daughter of a well–known Quaker minister, herself a twenty–four–year–old mother, taking from her household rag bag a clean scrap of cloth too small for a diaper for baby Elisha, fifteen months old and probably tugging at his mother's skirt, applying tallow to one side of the rag and bandaging the raw ends of the stubs of the two fingers of the now tamed "Bloody Tarleton." Then he "hastened back to the conflict." Tarleton rode the remainder of the morning battle and through the afternoon at the Courthouse battle with his hand bandaged and his arm in a sling. Did the blood–soaked bandage come from Hannah Coffin's bag of clean rags? Or was Hannah's patient really Colonel Tarleton? She never said. Perhaps she did not know; nor may we ever.

Colonel "Light Horse Harry" Lee also suffered a casualty at New Garden Meetinghouse, which though bloodless must have left a raw wound in the well–cultivated pride of the hard–bitten veteran of saddle warfare. Soon after the beginning of the battle his fiery chestnut sorrel became uncontrollably frightened and threw his young master to the ground. As Lee put it, "The sun had just risen above the trees, shining bright, the refulgence from the British muskets, as the soldiers presented, frightened Lee's horse so as to compel him to throw himself off." [104] This explanation may be a face–saving way out of an embarrassing situation, but it did not save his highly prized horse. It refused to obey the Colonel's order and fled from the battle:

> The horse ran to a stable about a mile from the place and unceremoniously took possession. Next morning, which was the morning after the battle, a man in the neighborhood, who had no standing in society, and no settled principles, but would do anything to catch a penny or ingratiate himself with those in power, learned where the horse was, went to the stable and got him, took him to the British camp at Martinville and sold him to Tarleton for a guinea or two.[105]

The only known relation of this story to Quakers is that it started from New Garden Meetinghouse, and Caruthers, who preserved it, said it came to him "from an old Quaker many years ago." [106] If anything could have hit Lee more embarrassingly than being thrown to the ground by his horse in the midst of a battle, it would have been the knowledge that his prized charger was being ridden by his hated rival, Banastre Tarleton.

Traditional accounts of the aftermath of the Battle of Guilford Courthouse often repeat a myth which has grown out of the use of the old New Garden Meetinghouse as a hospital. These accounts report that red finger prints could be clearly seen on the ceiling of the large frame meetinghouse which stood until the 1870s. For almost two hundred years these were fixed in the folklore of the people who knew about the meetinghouse. Often this frame meetinghouse was erroneously represented as the one used as a hospital for the soldiers wounded in the battles at New Garden and at Guilford Courthouse. A fascinating story told how these red finger prints got to the ceiling.

As the story goes, ceiling boards had been prepared for a new meetinghouse which was then in the planning stage. The log meetinghouse was not large enough to accommodate all the wounded, so some of the ceiling boards were spread upon the ground under the trees and wounded men laid upon them. The bloodstained fingers of these men left their prints in indelible red upon these boards. When the worship room was ceiled with these boards, the red finger prints were left to attract the attention of worshippers for the next eighty–five years. This story became firmly fixed in Quaker folklore for future generations.

A bit of research would have revealed reasons for doubting the fascinating tradition. The log meetinghouse in which the wounded were treated was destroyed by fire in 1784, three years after the battle. The frame meetinghouse with the fingerprinted ceiling boards was not erected until 1791. If the boards had been prepared in 1781 it seems doubtful that they could have been kept in good condition for the ten–year interval. Sixty years after the war some of the pupils of New Garden Boarding School asked Nathan Hunt, their "patron saint," about the authenticity of this story.

Nearly everyone seemed to accept the tradition without question. During the existence of the frame meetinghouse, the eyes of upward–looking worshippers were trapped and held by these would–be relics of the "day of solemnity and awfulness," as firmly fixed in the ceiling as stars in the heavens. Travelling ministers were enthralled by them and wrote the story, sometimes in garbled form, in their journals and diaries for succeeding generations to read and relate to children. No one seems to have asked why no large splotches were among the stains, which certainly would have been left by wounded men lying on the boards.

Two venerated members of the New Garden community left evidence which will give lovers of the fingerprint tradition a shock. In 1876 the old frame meetinghouse was sold to Albert Peele, a well–known Quaker minister at that time. He used the lumber in the construction of his house and barn. His son, Joseph Peele, who became as well loved and respected as his father, told me that as the ceiling boards were taken down it became clear that the red finger prints were not blood stains. In the first place, blood would not have retained the bright red color. The stains were from the hands of the carpenters who nailed the boards in place. In coloring the chalkline used in the process of straightening the edges of the boards, they had applied red chalk or powder. With some of this coloring material still on their hands, the carpenters had nailed the boards in place on the ceiling.

Before the building was torn down, young Will Boren, who became one of the best known citizens in the area, found evidence which refuted the bloodstain tradition. He told Katherine Hoskins that as a young man he went up into the gallery of the old meetinghouse to examine the finger prints at close range. He found some of the handprints extending across joints between boards: clear evidence that the prints were put there after the boards were put into place for nailing.

Some of the enthusiastic students of local history will experience pangs of sadness in the destruction of this myth. It was a good story. However, there is another tradition which bears some evidence of authenticity, and it may fill the void. The story came to me from Joe Durham, now well over a hundred years old. When he gave me the story, he was merely ninety–eight. His mind and memory were clear and his story convincing. His great aunt, Mary Ann Thornburg, born in 1836, told him that her grandmother gave the story to her. While the wounded soldiers were being treated in the old log meetinghouse large splotches of blood left their indelible stain on the floor. Despite repeated scrubbings with sand and soap, members of the meeting were unable to remove the stain which had seeped into the grain of the oak boards. The stains were in evidence only three years, since the building was destroyed by fire in 1784.

NATHANAEL GREENE AND NEW GARDEN QUAKERS

On March 26, 1781, Nathanael Greene wrote a letter to New Garden Friends. This missive has generally been overlooked and consequently it has been given little attention. It was written six days after General Greene left Guilford Courthouse in pursuit of Lord Cornwallis. At that time Greene must have been somewhere between Lindley's Mill on Cane Creek and the town of Pittsboro in Chatham County.

A hasty reading of the letter reveals a strong appeal to New Garden Friends for their help in caring for the large number of seriously wounded American and British soldiers whom the two armies had left at Guilford Courthouse. A superficial reading of the letter might make it seem to be a strong lecture to New Garden Friends on the basic issues of the war as the American general saw them. A careful reading of the communication gives convincing evidence in the light of events of a few preceding days that General Greene had another motive for writing to these Quakers at that time. A brief review of the events which transpired following the Battle of Guilford Courthouse provides necessary background for the letter, and particularly for an interpretation of the third part of it.

Before leaving Guilford County, Lord Cornwallis issued a proclamation to the people of the surrounding country which apparently caused General Greene a great deal of concern. In it, the British commander declared that the British army had won a signal victory at Guilford Courthouse and that the American army had been driven out of the country. The proclamation declared that the people of North Carolina should now return to their former allegiance to the British crown which alone could guarantee their liberties. It even offered amnesty to those who had taken part in the rebellion if they would surrender their arms and pledge their loyalty to the Crown.[107]

A brief wait would show that some of the boasts and promises made in the proclamation were empty, but at the time they were received by many people in the war–torn and war–weary population as a hopeful promise of relief. The war had been going on for nearly six years, and in much of North Carolina neither of the warring parties had provided a government able to maintain law and order. Bands of criminals had plagued the people of wide areas of the state and the Whigs and Tories had waged a pitiless guerilla war. The populace was tired of the terrible state of affairs and without a doubt many welcomed the proclamation in the hope that peace could now be restored.

General Greene's letter indicates that there must have been more than one proclamation. Brief accounts of the progress of the British army through areas which were thought to be strongly Loyalist indicate that Cornwallis made several appeals to the people along the way to join his force and support his effort to restore stable government. For several weeks before the Battle of Guilford Courthouse, the rival commanders had waged a vigorous psychological battle for the minds and support of the people of the interior of North Carolina. It had been expected that the Battle of Guilford Courthouse would settle this issue. Actually it did not, although for a short time the result seemed to favor the British, and Cornwallis took advantage of it.

In the days following the issue of the proclamation, General Greene's reactions showed us that he was uneasy about the developments, and he took energetic steps to counter the propaganda which Cornwallis was scattering over the country. His hope was to prevent war–weary people from surrendering their minds and support to it. One of the first opportunities to act came when the Marquis of Malmedy led his company of mounted militia to General Greene. The American commander sent this force to screen the advance of the

British army and to convince the people along the way that the American army was still a force to be reckoned with.

Greene's next move was a more effective one. Before he led the main body of his army through the South Buffalo Creek area toward Cane Creek, he sent two of his most skillful military leaders to hang onto the rear and flanks of the retreating British army. On this mission Colonel Henry Lee had his usual, strong force of cavalry and light infantry. Colonel William Washington had his full cavalry unit. At every opportunity they were to pounce upon any bands or individuals who ventured beyond the protection of the camp or main body of the British army, cut down foragers, and embarrass the enemy in every possible way. Above all they were to convince the people along the way that the American army was still strong and intact and that the British army was actually running away from the Americans. As Colonel Lee stated their purpose, General Greene:

> . . .detached lieutenant colonel Lee with his legion and militia rifle corps under Campbell to hang on the rear of the retreating general, lest the inhabitants of the region through which he passed presume that our army had been rendered incapable of further resistance and might flock to the royal standard.[108]

Here in brief is General Greene's burning fear and the effective step which he was taking to counter British propaganda. This statement also shows that Colonel Lee's force was of considerable strength.

Colonel Washington, at the head of his cavalry, was on a similar mission. He and Colonel Lee were rough on Tories who had been with the British or who were found making any move to join them:

> Before they [i.e., the British] left Bell's Mill on the morning of the 21st Lee and Washington were hovering near cutting off stragglers, occasionally they hung a murdering Tory.[109]

Caruthers leaves an animated example of the way Colonel Washington dealt with the people who were not Tories but showed an inclination to respond to the recent British propaganda. While scouting with a group of his cavalrymen near the British camp at Bell's Mill, he saw a group of thirty or more men approaching from a distance. He ordered his men to a place of concealment, where they could watch while the unknown men approached him. The broad hats of the strangers indicated to Washington that they were Quakers. They were from the Back Creek, Carraway, and Uwharrie areas of Randolph County. Not expecting to see an American soldier so near the British army at Bell's Mill, they addressed Washington as a British soldier. The American colonel made no effort to reveal his true identity. Instead, he opened the way for these Quakers to talk to him freely as a British soldier:

> They told him that Greene had been defeated and driven out of the county, or obliged to retreat to Rockingham [county], the British arms were now completely triumphant, that they were going to pay their respects to friend Cornwallis, and tell him they were peace–loving, sober, quiet people, having no enmity toward him or the British Government. [110]

This interpretation of recent events is exactly what Cornwallis hoped would come from his proclamation, and it is certainly what Greene feared would come from it.

It is not surprising that Quakers from Randolph County were on their way to assure Cornwallis that they would abide by a restored colonial government. In the first place, Quakers were in the habit of abiding by the rule of the established government so long as it did not require them to violate what they considered the will of God. Their section of Randolph County had been an area of some of the worst of the Tory–Whig conflict. The lives and property of the Quakers had often been in jeopardy. They were tired of atrocities, lawlessness, and a lack of effective government. The Quaker told Charles Stedman, the British historian, ". . . the people have experienced such distress that I believe they would submit to any government in the world to obtain peace." [111] The propaganda which Cornwallis had been spreading must have seemed to them the harbinger of a period in which order might be restored. They were on their way to Bell's Mill to tell Cornwallis that they welcomed the restoration of peace.

Colonel Washington allowed these unsuspecting Quakers to talk freely before revealing his identity. He then ordered his cavalry to appear and surround the whole group while he gave them a stern lecture. Before telling them to go home and live by the principles of their faith, he ordered six of the best dressed of them to exchange clothing from "top to toe" with six of his men "whose regimentals had become the most shabby looking." Then he ordered a similar exchange of horses.[112] Caruthers says that long after the war Quaker tradition kept alive the picture of well–known Friends,[113] perhaps some of them elders and overseers, dressed in worn out cavalry uniforms and astride jaded cavalry horses returning home to the astonished looks of their families. It must have been equally strange to see men of the cavalry of Colonel Washington, dressed in Quaker hats and coats, charging down upon a British foraging party with drawn swords and blazing guns.

Colonel Washington's *rencontre* with the Randolph County Quakers occurred four or five days before General Greene wrote his letter to the New Garden Friends — plenty of time for him to have received reports from his two cavalry commanders. Washington must have given Greene a full report of his encounter with the Randolph County Quakers: how they were interpreting recent events and particularly their unquestioning acceptance of Cornwallis's propaganda. The response of the Quakers to the proclamation of Cornwallis would impress Greene more than the ludicrous aspects of their meeting with Washington. Certainly they were not the only people to react in this way to the British overtures.

When Greene wrote to the New Garden Friends, the British and American armies were approximately fifty miles from Guilford Courthouse, with little prospect that either would ever return. However, it was still important to the cause of independence that loyalist sentiment be controlled in that section as well as in other parts of the state. Apparently, Greene was determined to maintain a counteroffensive for just such a reason. He knew that the New Garden Quakers were influential people in the Guilford County area, and so the letter was written:

> To the members of New Garden Monthly Meeting near Guilford Court House:
>
> Friends and Countrymen: I address myself to your humanity for the relief of the suffering wounded at Guilford Court House. As a people I am persuaded you disclaim any connection with measures calculated to promote military operations; but I know of no order of men more remarkable for the exercise of humanity and benevolence; and perhaps no instance ever had a higher claim upon you than the unfortunate wounded in your neighborhood.[114]

Later in the letter he said, "Having given you this information, I have only to remark that I shall be exceedingly obliged to you to contribute all in your power to relieve the unfortunates at Guilford."[115] It was an eloquent and touching appeal, and no doubt the seriously wounded whom he had left at Guilford Courthouse (possibly more than two hundred in all) were weighing heavily upon his mind and conscience.

Other paragraphs in the letter indicate, however, that the major purpose of the letter was to counteract any influence which Cornwallis's proselytizing might be having in the area. In the second paragraph of the letter the erstwhile Friend tells of his Quaker background and expresses his appreciation for the Society of Friends:

I was born and educated in the profession and principles of your Society; and am perfectly acquainted with your religious sentiments and general good conduct as citizens. I am also sensible from the prejudices of many belonging to other religious societies, and the misconduct of a few of your own, that you are generally considered as enemies of the independence of America. I entertain other sentiments, both of your principles and wishes. I respect you as a people, and shall always be ready to protect you from violence and oppression which the confusion of the times afford but too many instances of.[116]

This paragraph seems to be an introduction to what is, perhaps, the major concern of the American general, a reply to the British propaganda:

Do not be deceived. This is no religious dispute. The contest is for political liberty without which cannot be enjoyed the free exercise of your religion.

The British are flattering you with conquest and exciting your apprehensions respecting religious liberty. They deceive you in both. They can neither conquer this country, nor will you be molested in the exercise of your sentiments. It is true they may spread desolation and distress over many parts of the country, but when the inhabitants exert their force, the enemy must flee before them. There is but one way to put a speedy end to the extremities of war, which is, for the people to be united. It is the interest of your enemy to create divisions among you, and while they prevail your distress will continue. Look at the horrid misorders among the Whigs and Tories. Have the enemy any friends to suffer or feel for? They have not neither do they care how great your calamities if it but contributes to the gratification of their pride and ambition. You

would neither have liberty nor property could the enemy succeed in
their measures. How they have deceived you in their proclamations?
and how have they violated their faith with your friends in South
Carolina? They are now fleeing before us, and must soon be expelled
from our land if the people will continue to aid the operations of the
army.[117]

Here in one paragraph is General Greene's strong refutation of the
propaganda which Cornwallis had been spreading across the country
as he retreated by stages toward Wilmington. It is an eloquent statement couched in strong language and backed by the most forceful
arguments which Greene could muster. He was attempting to do by
letter what Colonels Lee and Washington had been doing by military
force, tongue lashings, and hangings. No doubt he expected the
contents of the letter to reach most of the Quakers in Guilford County
and through them many other people who were not members of the
Society of Friends.

The letter by New Garden Friends written in reply to that of
General Greene was brief, strong in word power, and rich in content.
The major portion of it relates to the efforts made by New Garden
Friends to care for the numerous wounded soldiers, thrown into their
care by the British and American armies as they hastened from that part
of the country. The last sentence may be interpreted as their response
to Greene's eloquent argument against the British and his warning to
New Garden Friends not to succumb to Cornwallis's influence. The
last sentence also illustrates their unfaltering defense of the Quaker
stand against war, and in it there is what appears to be a rebuke of the
General for his effort to pressure them to comply with his request:

To Major General Nathanael Greene:

Friend Greene: We received thine, being dated March 20, 1781.
Agreeable to thy request we shall do all that lies in our power,
although this may inform you that from our present situation we are
ill able to assist as much as we would be glad to do, as the Americans
have lain much upon us, and of late the British have plundered and
entirely broken up many among us, which renders it hard, and there
is at our meeting–house at New Garden upward of one hundred now
living, that have no means of provision, except what hospitality the
neighborhood affords them, which we look upon as a hardship upon
us, if not an imposition; but not withstanding all this, we are
determined, by the assistance of Providence, while we have any-

thing among us, that the distressed both at the court house and here shall have part with us. As we have as yet made no distinction as to party or cause — and as we have none to commit our cause but to God alone, but hold it the duty of true Christians, at all times to assist the distressed.

Guilford Court House, N. C. Third Mo. 31,1781.[118]

The letter makes some revelations not found in any other source. How had the "Americans lain much upon" them? Or is this a reference to Greene's leaving more than two hundred of those wounded at Guilford Courthouse and asking the Quakers to assume a major part of the responsibility? It also reveals that after the Battle of Guilford Courthouse, the British had foraged the resources of the New Garden Quakers to the bone, leaving many of them destitute. Two weeks after the battle around one hundred wounded men were still being cared for at the meetinghouse. How many had died there is not revealed, but there is one strange oversight: no reference is made to the many sick and wounded soldiers who were treated in the homes of New Garden Friends.

One phrase implies that the New Garden Friends looked upon this burden as an "imposition." This is not surprising. They knew that the care of the wounded was the responsibility of the military forces. Under pressure of the exigencies of war, both armies had run away from this responsibility and had thrown a tremendous burden upon people in the area after foragers of the two armies had already stripped them of their resources. In spite of everything New Garden Friends said, ". . . we are determined by the assistance of Providence . . . to share with the . . . distressed at the court house and here."

Not to be swayed by the propaganda which Cornwallis had been spreading nor to give their support to the Loyalist cause, New Garden Friends told Greene that they had "made no distinction as to party or cause." This was stating a long standing position taken by Friends in wartime. As it applied to the Revolutionary War, they would make no distinction between Tory and Whig or between independence or British Empire. Caring for the wounded was another matter and in both sides would receive their care.

In the last sentence of their letter the New Garden Friends seem to give General Greene a forceful rebuke. Greene had concluded his letter with a strong plea for assistance in the care of the wounded: "from the liberality of your order upon the occasion I shall be able to indulge your feelings as men and principles as a Society." If this was an attempt on the part of the general to pressure New Garden Friends to act favorably on his request, it boomeranged. It exposed him to a sharp reply: "We have none to submit our cause to but God alone."[119] No former Quaker, not even a commanding major general, could shake them from the bedrock of their faith: reliance on God's leadership, mercy, and approbation. They spurned Nathanael Greene as the judge of their actions.

While Greene was writing his letter to New Garden Friends, Cornwallis was beginning to move his army across Deep River at Ramsey's Mill to evade the battle anticipated by the American general. The battle was never fought. When Cornwallis pushed his army across Deep River and through the unresponsive Tory country around Cross Creek, Greene gave up the pursuit and marched into South Carolina for an attempt to free that state of British occupation. Even if anyone in Guilford County had wanted to make any move to support the British cause, there was now no British army in the area to join. The propaganda battle had ended by default.

When Cornwallis reached Wilmington, he effected a rehabilitation of his army and then marched to Yorktown, Virginia, where he surrendered to George Washington on October 19, 1781. This virtually ended the fighting in the Revolutionary War. A few Whigs and Tories in North Carolina kept up their skirmishes and depredations for more than a year after the surrender at Yorktown.

SIGNIFICANCE OF THE BATTLE

The significance of the Battle of New Garden is a subject which clings to speculation. It may be sought in the cumulative effect of the numerous clashes between the Americans and British in the long exhaustive campaign which reached from South Carolina to Virginia and continued for another month in a wide arena in the northern part of the North Carolina Piedmont. It has been estimated that there were 137 encounters of various degrees of force and intensity in this long campaign. The cumulative effect of these encounters make this midwinter struggle appear to be a war of attrition. In it the British suffered more than the Americans. In this long struggle, the Battle of

Guilford Courthouse was the major battle toward which the whole campaign had moved. After the conflict, the *Annual Register* made what may be called an English evaluation of the effect of the numerous minor conflicts in the war:

> Most of these actions would in other wars be considered as skirmishes of little account, and scarcely worthy of detailed narrative. But these small actions are as capable as any in displaying military conduct. The operations of war being spread over a vast continent, by the new plan that was adopted, it is by such skirmishes that the fate of America must necessarily be decided. They are therefore as important as battles.[120]

Seen in the light of the competence of its leaders, the number and quality of the soldiers involved, the duration and intensity of the fighting, and the number of casualties, the Battle of New Garden stands out as one of the most important of the 137 conflicts in this campaign. It may also be placed in the class of the most important of the minor battles of the Revolutionary War in North Carolina such as Moore's Creek Bridge, Ramsours Mill, Elizabethtown, and Lindley's Mill. Its effect on the Battle of Guilford Courthouse is hidden in the degree to which it sapped the strength of the British force. It delayed the Battle of Guilford Courthouse for several hours and must have contributed to the fatigue of a high percentage of the British army. The entire British army marched and fought throughout the day without food. The casualties of the morning, the ensuing delay, and the increased fatigue are believed to have been more detrimental to the British than to the Americans. The delay which the battle introduced into the progress of the British army toward Guilford Courthouse gave General Greene ample time to make necessary preparations for the battle and to rest and feed the seven–eighths of his army not engaged in the morning battle, while the remainder fought about one–fourth of the British army. The other three–fourths of the British force was on the road without food. Although there is no way of measuring the effects, all of these considerations lead to the conclusion that the Battle of New Garden militated to the benefit of the Americans at Guilford Courthouse. There can be little question about the effects of the morning battle and the Battle of Guilford Courthouse upon the Quakers of the New Garden community: first a shock, then a tremendous burden, followed by an agonizing memory.

ENDNOTES

[1] Rev. E. W. Caruthers, D.D., *Interesting Revolutionary Incidents: And Sketches of Character, Chiefly in the "Old North State."* 2nd ser. (Philadelphia: Hayes & Zell, 1856), p. 150.

[2] William Seymour, *A Journal of the Southern Expedition 1780–1783* (Wilmington, DE: the Historical Society of Delaware, 1896), p. 20.

[3] Walter Clark, ed., *State Records of North Carolina*, 26 vols. (Goldsboro: Nash Brothers, 1905), v. 17:1001.

[4] Banastre Tarleton, *A History of the Campaigns of 1780–1781, in the Southern Provinces of North America*, Dublin: Printed for Colles, etc., 1787), p. 246.

[5] Henry Lee, *The Campaign of 1781 in the Carolinas; With Remarks on Johnson's Life of Greene* (Philadelphia: E. Littell, 1824), p. 146.

[6] Hugh F. Rankin, *The North Carolina Continentals* (Chapel Hill: University of North Carolina Press, 1971), p. 279.

[7] *The Annual Register, or View of the History, Politics and Literature of the Year 1781* (London: Dodsley, 1782), p. 65.

[8] Addison Coffin, "Pioneer Days in Guilford County," *The Guilford Collegian* 3, No. 9 (May 1891): 230.

[9] This information was given me in 1940 by John Gurney Frazier, Sr.

[10] Speedwell Ironworks was located on Troublesome Creek in Rockingham County. By the roads of that day it was variously estimated to be fifteen to twenty miles from Guilford Courthouse.

[11] Charles D. Caldwell, *Memoirs of the Life and Campaigns of the Hon. Nathaniel [sic] Greene* (Philadelphia: Robert Desilver, 1819), p. 181.

[12] Colonel William Washington, the other calvary leader in Greene's army, was kept at Guilford Courthouse with the main body of the American army.

[13] Lucien Agniel, *The Late Affair Has Almost Broke My Heart: The American Revolution in the South, 1780–1781* (Riverside, CT: The Chatham Press, Inc., 1972), pp. 31–32.

[14] For a brief description of the young colonel, see Burke Davis, *The Cowpens–Guilford Courthouse Campaign* (Philadelphia and New York: J. B. Lippincott Company, 1962), p. 26.

[15] *Ibid.*

[16] Agniel, *American Revolution in the South,* pp. 35–36.

[17] Sidney George Fisher, *The Struggle for American Independence,* 2 vols. (Philadelphia and London: J. B. Lippincott Company, 1908), 2:271.

[18] The uniforms of the opposing cavalrymen were strikingly similar; both wore green coats. This is the reason why Colonel Pyle's men thought they were being attacked by the British cavalry.

[19] Davis, *Guilford Courthouse Campaign,* p. 110.

[20] Franklin and Mary Wickwire, *Cornwallis: The American Adventure* (Boston: Houghton Mifflin Company, 1970), p. 293.

[21] David Schenck, *North Carolina 1780–81* (Raleigh: Edwards and Broughton, Publishers, 1889), p. 314.

[22] Addison Coffin, "The Battle of Guilford Court House," *The Guilford Collegian* 4, No. 6 (February 1892): 133.

[23] Preston's name is given in different places as "James," "John" and "William." See Rankin, *North Carolina Continentals,* p. 295, and Schenck, *North Carolina 1780–81,* pp. 277 and 311.

[24] Henry Lee, *Memoirs of the War in the Southern Department of the United States* (Washington, DC: Printed by Peter Force, 1827), p. 169, gives only "Captain Armstrong." It is not known if he was "John" or "Martin" Armstrong.

[25] These estimates are found in Lee, *Memoirs,* p. 158, and Schenck, *North Carolina 1780–81,* pp. 302, 307, 311 and 325.

[26] Tarleton, *History of Campaigns,* p. 241.

[27] *Ibid.,* p. 277.

[28] "General Orders, 14th March, 1781"; See Caruthers, *Revolutionary Incidents,* pp. 435–36.

[29] Lee, *Memoirs,* p. 170.

[30] Dr. and Mrs. Warren Ashby, of the University of North Carolina at Greensboro, in the summer of 1975, saw in the British Museum an exhibit on the "American Rebellion." It included a copy of Mouzon's map of North and South Carolina as one used by Cornwallis.

[31] Letter to Lord Germain, dated "17th March, 1781." See John H. Wheeler, *Historical Sketches of North Carolina, From 1584 to 1851* (Philadelphia: Lippincott, Grambo and Company, 1851), p. 177.

[32] Lee, *Memoirs,* p. 182.

[33] Tarleton, *History of Campaigns,* p. 286.

[34] Schenck, *North Carolina 1780–81,* p. 358.

[35] *Ibid.,* p. 357.

[36] Lee, *Memoirs,* p. 166.

[37] Schenck, *North Carolina 1780–81,* p. 292.

[38] Benson Lossing, *Pictorial Field Book of the Revolution,* 2 vols. (New York: Harper Brothers, 1855) 2:400.

[39] Caruthers, *Revolutionary Incidents,* p. 435. For locations of McCuiston, see Lossing, *Pictorial Field Book,* p. 800.

[40] Wheeler, *Historical Sketches,* p. 172; and Tarleton, *History of Campaigns,* pp. 274–275.

[41] Tarleton, *History of Campaigns,* p. 246.

[42] Lee, *Memoirs,* p. 166.

[43] *Order Book* of Cornwallis. See Caruthers, *Revolutionary Incidents,* p. 435.

[44] *Ibid.*

[45] Mary Mendenhall Hobbs, "Nereus Mendenhall," *Quaker Biographies,* 2nd Ser. (Philadelphia: Friends' Book Store, n.d.), 5:250–51.

[46] Caruthers, *Revolutionary Incidents,* p. 153.

[47] The second letter of Lord Cornwallis to Lord Germain, dated March 17, 1781, relative to events prior to the Battle of Guilford Courthouse. See Tarleton, *History of Campaigns,* p. 274.

[48] Tarleton, *History of Campaigns,* p. 277.

[49] Wheeler, *Historical Sketches,* p. 177.

[50] *Ibid.,* p. 175.

[51] *Ibid.,* p. 175–176.

[52] Addison Coffin, "Battle of Guilford Court House," p. 133.

[53] Wheeler, *Historical Sketches,* pp. 175–76.

[54] Caruthers, *Revolutionary Incidents,* p. 155.

[55] Seymour, *Journal of Southern Expedition,* p. 20.

[56] Lee, *Memoirs, p. 168.*

[57] Tarleton, *History of Campaigns,* p. 278.

[58] Lee, *Memoirs,* p. 168.

[59] *Ibid.,* p. 169.

[60] *Ibid.*

[61] The tradition about the location of this road was given by John Gurney Frazier, Sr., in 1940. He was then eighty–four. He had heard it when he

was a young man.

[62] Lee, *Memoirs,* p. 169.

[63] *Ibid.,* p. 170.

[64] *Ibid.*

[65] *Ibid.*

[66] *Ibid.*

[67] *Ibid.*

[68] Wickwire, *Cornwallis,* p. 294; and Schenck, *North Carolina 1780–81,* p. 382.

[69] Lee, *Memoirs,* p. 170.

[70] Levi Coffin, *Reminiscences of Levi Coffin,* 2nd ed. (Cincinnati: Robert Clarke & Co., 1880), pp. 9–10.

[71] During the past twenty years gravediggers have dug up parts of human skeletons in two areas of the present New Garden cemetery: two graves near the eastern border and one above the lowland of the northwestern corner. These areas must have been in the woods near the cemetery in 1781.

[72] Lee, *Memoirs,* p. 170, n.

[73] Captain James Tate's remains were removed from the New Garden cemetery to Guilford Courthouse Park soon after it was established in 1888. See John W. Albright, *Greensboro, 1808–1904, Facts, Figures, Traditions and Reminiscences* (Greensboro: Jos. J. Stone & Company, 1904), p. 111.

[74] Lee, *Memoirs,* p. 170.

[75] Charles Stedman, *The History of the Origin, Processes and Termination of the American War,* 2 vols. (London: Printed by the author, 1974), 2: 370; and Lee, *Memoirs,* p. 170.

[76] New Garden Boarding School was founded in 1837, fifty–six years after the battle.

[77] This was written after Guilford College was founded.

[78] Addison Coffin, "A Letter from Addison Coffin," *The Guilford Collegian* 1, No. 2 (February 1889): 40–41. This article, signed "L. H. H." (it should be L. L. H. — Lewis Lyndon Hobbs, President of Guilford College), consists of several extracts from Coffin's letter to Dr. Hobbs.

[79] Tarleton, *History of Campaigns,* p. 278.

[80] Addison Coffin, "Battle of Guilford Court House," p. 133.

[81] Stedman, *History of American Wars,* p. 337.

[82] See "Letter from Addison Coffin." Coffin is quoted as saying that ". . . widow Juda Russell lived" in this house and that John M. Morehead (later Governor of North Carolina) and James T. Morehead, "when young men boarded with Juda Russell and attended Andrew Caldwell's Latin School" (p. 40).

[83] Lee, *Memoirs*, p. 180.

[84] Tarleton, *History of Campaigns*, p. 286.

[85] See Caruthers, *Revolutionary Incidents*, p. 440, for the order by Cornwallis.

[86] Tarleton, *History of Campaigns*, p. 287.

[87] See map given after the title page in Caruthers, *Revolutionary Incidents*.

[88] Annette G. Way, "Nathan Hunt," *Quaker Biographies*, 2nd ser. (Philadelphia: Friends' Book Store, n.d.), 1: 166.

[89] Charles Coffin, *The Life of Elijah Coffin: With Reminiscences* (Cincinnati: E. Morgan and Sons, 1863), pp. 11–12.

[90] *Ibid.*, p. 12

[91] See the Minutes of New Garden Monthly Meeting for that date. The Minutes are in the Quaker Collection in the Library of Guilford College.

[92] Davis, *Guilford Courthouse Campaign*, p. 54, and other pages interspersed in the book.

[93] Rufus M. Jones, *The Quakers in the American Colonies* (London: Macmillan and Co., Ltd., 1911; rpt. New York: Russell and Russell, 1962), pp. 296 and 337–38.

[94] Addison Coffin, "Battle of Guilford Court House," p. 137.

[95] This information was given me by the gravedigger who on two occasions showed me the graves where the human bones were unearthed. These visits to the graves were in August 1975.

[96] Tarleton, *History of Campaigns*, p. 286.

[97] Wickwire, *Cornwallis*, p. 314.

[98] James Graham, *The Life of General Daniel Morgan of the Virginia Line of the United States* (New York: Derby & Jackson, 1856), p. 372.

[99] Caldwell, *Memoirs of N. Greene Campaigns*, p. 245.

[100] Levi Coffin, *Reminiscences*, p. 10. Richard Williams was an ancestor of J. Edgar Williams, the first full–time pastor of New Garden Meeting. His wife, Prudence Beals Williams, was a sister of Phebe Beals Sumner, who with her husband lived in the New Garden community at the time of the battle. The Sumners were ancestors of Eva Miles Newlin, now a member of New Garden Meeting. New Garden records show that six of

Prudence Beals Williams twelve children (five girls and one boy) were under eighteen years of age at the time.

[101] Way, *Quaker Biographies,* p. 166.

[102] Wickwire, *Cornwallis,* p. 294.

[103] Charles Coffin, *Elijah Coffin,* p. 12.

[104] Lee, *Memoirs,* p. 170.

[105] Caruthers, *Revolutionary Incidents,* p. 154.

[106] *Ibid.,* p. 155.

[107] Stedman, *History of American Wars,* p. 351; and Tarleton, *History of Campaigns,* pp. 286–87.

[108] Lee, *Memoirs,* p. 181.

[109] Caruthers, *Revolutionary Incidents,* p. 176.

[110] *Ibid.,* p. 179.

[111] Stedman, *History of American Wars,* p. 348.

[112] Caruthers, *Revolutionary Incidents,* p. 180.

[113] *Ibid.,* p. 181.

[114] Philips Russell, *North Carolina in the Revolutionary War* (Charlotte, NC: Heritage Company, 1965), p. 222.

[115] *Ibid.*

[116] *Ibid.*

[117] *Ibid.*

[118] *Ibid.*

[119] *Ibid. Both* letters are given on pp. 222–23.

[120] *The Annual Register 1781,* p. 65.

WORKS CITED

Agniel, Lucien. *The Late Affair Has Almost Broke My Heart: The American Revolution in the South, 1780–1781.* Riverside, CT: The Chatham Press, 1972.

Albright, John W. *Greensboro, 1808–1904, Facts, Figures, Traditions and Reminiscences.* Greensboro: Jos. J. Stone & Company, 1904.

The Annual Register, or View of the History, Politics and Literature of the Year 1781. London: Dodsley, 1782.

Caldwell, Charles. *Memoirs of the Life and Campaigns of the Hon. Nathaniel [sic] Greene.* Philadelphia: Robert Desilver, 1819.

Caruthers, Rev. E. W. *Interesting Revolutionary Incidents: And Sketches of Character, Chiefly in the "Old North State."* 2nd ser. Philadelphia: Hayes & Zell, 1856.

Coffin, Addison. "The Battle of Guilford Court House." *The Guilford Collegian* 4, No. 6 (February 1892): 133–37.

_____. "A Letter From Addison Coffin." *The Guilford Collegian* 1, No. 2 (February 1889): 40–41.

_____. "Pioneer Days in Guilford County." *The Guilford Collegian* 3, No. 9 (May 1891): 230–22.

Coffin, Charles. *The Life of Elijah Coffin: With Reminiscences.* Cincinnati: E. Morgan and Sons, 1863.

Coffin, Elijah. "Friends of North Carolina." *Friends' Review* 14, No. 37 (Fifth Month 1861): 580–81.

Coffin, Levi. *Reminiscences of Levi Coffin.* 2nd ed. Cincinnati: Robert Clarke & Company, 1880.

Davis, Burke. *The Cowpens–Guilford Courthouse Campaign.* Philadelphia and London: J. B. Lippincott Company, 1962.

Fisher, Sidney George. *The Struggle for American Independence.* 2 vols. Philadelphia and London: J. B. Lippincott Company, 1908.

Graham, James. *The Life of General Daniel Morgan of the Virginia Line of the United States, With Portions of His Correspondence Compiled from Authentic Sources.* New York: Derby & Jackson, 1856.

Hobbs, Mary Mendenhall. "Nereus Mendenhall," *Quaker Biographies.* 2nd ser. 5 vols. Philadelphia: Friends' Book Store, n.d., 5: 245–305.

Johnson, William. *Sketches of the Life and Correspondences of Nathanael Greene, in the War of the Revolution.* 2 vols. Charleston, SC: A. E. Miller, 1822.

Jones, Rufus M. *The Quakers in the American Colonies.* London: Macmillan and Co., Ltd., 1911; rpt. New York: Russell and Russell, 1962.

Lee, Henry. *Memoirs of the War in the Southern Department of the United States.* Washington, DC. Printed by Peter Force, 1827.

_____. *Campaign of 1781 in the Carolinas; With Remarks Historical and Critical on Johnson's Life of Greene.* Philadelphia: E. Littell, 1824.

Lossing, Benson. *Pictorial Field Book of the Revolution; Or Illustrations by Pen and Pencil of the History, Biography, Scenery, Relics and Traditions of the War of Independence.* 2 vols. New York: Harper and Brothers, 1855.

Rankin, Hugh F. *The North Carolina Continentals.* Chapel Hill: University of North Carolina Press, 1971.

Russell, Phillips. *North Carolina in the Revolutionary War.* Charlotte, NC: Heritage Company, 1965.

Schenck, David. *North Carolina 1780–81.* Raleigh: Edwards and Broughton, Publishers, 1889.

Seymour, William. *A Journal of the Southern Expedition 1780–1783.* Wilmington, DE: The Historical Society of Delaware, 1896.

Stedman, Charles. *The History of the Origin, Progress and Termination of the American War.* 2 vols. London: Printed by the Author, 1794.

Tarleton, Banastre. *A History of the Campaigns of 1780–1781, in the Southern Provinces of North America.* Dublin: Printed for Colles etc., 1787.

Way, Annette G. "Nathan Hunt." *Quaker Biographies.* 2nd ser. 5 vols. Philadelphia: Friends' Book Store, n.d., 1: 155–86.

Wheeler, John H. *Historical Sketches of North Carolina. From 1584 to 1851.* Philadelphia: Lippincott, Grambo and Company, 1851.

Wickwire, Franklin and Mary. *Cornwallis: The American Adventure.* Boston: Houghton Mifflin Company, 1970.

ACKNOWLEDGMENTS

I am grateful to Dr. Edward F. Burrows and Dr. Alexander R. Stoesen, both of Guilford College. They have read this manuscript at different stages of its development and have given many helpful suggestions.

I am grateful to members of the staff of the Guilford College Library and especially grateful to Treva W. Mathis, Curator of the Quaker Collection,* for the assistance given me during my research. Nearly all of the material for this treatise came from the Guilford College Library; much of it from the Quaker Collection.

My sincere thanks go to Herbert Poole, Library Director of Guilford College, for his careful work in editing the manuscript, to Jo Poole and Rose Simon for their assistance in this work, to Nancy Settlemyre for typing the manuscript, and to Fred Hughes for his careful and highly professional work on the maps of the battle area.

Algie I. Newlin
1977

Reprint editor's note: now called the Friends Historical Collection.